SHOES AND PATTENS

OBITUARY

Margrethe de Neergaard, 1953–1987

Margrethe de Neergaard died in August 1987, at
the tragically early age of 34, just as this book
was going to press. She had been seriously
ill for several years, and it is a tribute
to her bravery, determination and sheer
enthusiasm for the subject that despite partial
disability she was able to bring those sections
for which she was chiefly responsible –
Shoemaking and Cobbling
and *Shoes in Art and Literature* –
to a state close to completion.

MEDIEVAL FINDS FROM EXCAVATIONS IN LONDON: 2

SHOES AND PATTENS

Francis Grew and Margrethe de Neergaard

Illustrations by Susan Mitford

LONDON · HER MAJESTY'S STATIONERY OFFICE

ISBN 0 11 290443 2

KEY
(For further explanation of the terms used see Glossary, pp. 123–5)

○   ○   ○   ○   Grain/flesh stitching

●   ●   ●   ●   Edge/flesh stitching

Binding-stitch

Tunnel-stitching

Reinforcement cord

Printed in the United Kingdom for Her Majesty's Stationery Office
Dd. 240055 4/88 C20 31658

Contents

Acknowledgements

Eight of the ten excavations which produced the shoes described in this volume were financed by the Department of the Environment (whose responsibility has recently been transferred to the Historic Buildings and Monuments Commission), as was nearly all the post-excavation analysis. The excavations at Swan Lane and Ludgate Hill were generously sponsored by Edger Investments Limited and the Norwich Union Insurance Group respectively. Additional grants were received from the Corporation of the City of London and the Manpower Services Commission (Billingsgate), and from the Museum of London Trust Fund and the City of London Archaeological Trust (Swan Lane and Billingsgate). Individual thanks are due to Jane Cowgill, Penny MacConnoran and Quita Mould for carrying out much of the initial recording; to Helen Ganiaris, Rose Johnson, Suzanne Keene and Katharine Starling of the Museum's Conservation Laboratory; to Alan Eddy (British Museum, Natural History), Glynis Edwards (Ancient Monuments Laboratory) and Rowena Gale for providing specialist reports on the moss stuffing, leather and wood; to Neil MacDonald (C. & J. Clark Ltd.) and Claire Symonds (Shoe and Allied Trades Research Association) for information about modern shoes; to Dominique Vaughan and Friedericke Hammer for providing summaries in French and German respectively; to Jon Bailey, Trevor Hurst and Jan Scrivener of the Museum's Photographic Department; to John Cherry, John Clark, Tony Dyson, Geoff Egan, Olaf Goubitz, Arthur MacGregor, Michael Rhodes, Frances Pritchard, Erik Schia, Brian Spencer, June Swann, Roy Thompson, Alan Vince and Willy Groenman-van Waateringe for making many improvements and contributions to the text; and, finally, to Fred Stubbs and the staff of Her Majesty's Stationery Office for skilfully turning the manuscripts into print.

Introduction

The subject of the second fascicule in the Museum of London's series on recent medieval finds from the City is one to which archaeology in Britain has previously made very little contribution. Medieval shoes, boots and pattens, being made of leather or wood, are rarely preserved on sites, and their appearance is normally inferred from such sources as manuscript illustrations, monumental effigies and brasses, or contemporary writings. The recovery of well over a thousand examples, many of them complete and in almost perfect condition, is thus an achievement of great significance; both for the information they can provide about details of construction, decoration or fashion and, above all, because they come from a continuous series of deposits datable to within half a century or less, for evidence about the evolution of different styles and their relative popularity.

Leather can survive only in anaerobic conditions and London's large collection of medieval footwear is the product of an unusually high proportion of thick organic deposits which have often been encountered during excavation or rebuilding, especially along the riverfront. By 1970 the shoe collection already totalled about a hundred, split equally between the Guildhall and the London Museums, but since it was not published in detail in any of the pre-War catalogues (Guildhall Museum 1903; London Museum 1935; 1940) it remained virtually unknown except to those who had been able to examine it at first hand. The collection is still of value, for it contains some types that have not been found subsequently (see, for example, below, p. 119), but it has been dwarfed by the discoveries of the past fourteen years, which are the subject of the present volume and have the additional advantage of coming from closely-dated levels.

By good fortune the 1970s and 1980s, the first period of large-scale rescue archaeology in London, have coincided with the availability through redevelopment of a series of enormous sites on the north bank of the Thames where, equally by good fortune, the medieval population of the City continually reclaimed land by building timber revetments ever further into the river and filling the space behind them with common domestic rubbish. The rubbish was evidently collected from streets and households throughout London (see Rhodes, in Milne & Milne 1982, 86–8) and was dumped immediately, so that normally there is a direct link with a particular revetment, itself often dated by dendrochronology, and a much lower chance than usual of a given layer – which in turn may contain datable pottery and coins – being contaminated with residual material (for details of dating, see Appendix I, pp. 131–6). The chronological limits of this volume, c.1100–1450, thus correspond exactly with the main period of reclamation, a process which came to an end with the construction of stone walls along much of the riverfront. Saxo-Norman footwear, both from the clay banks which preceded the timber wharves and from pits in the interior of the City, is to be described in a comprehensive survey of all London finds of this date (Pritchard forthcoming), while the only substantial 16th-century group will probably be included in a full report on the Tudor Baynards Castle with which it was associated.

The task of publishing nearly one thousand five hundred medieval shoes in a form that is both comprehensive and easy to handle is a formidable one. A catalogue of every example, complete or incomplete, is clearly ruled out on grounds of length and cost, and, in any case, the more one examines the collection the more it becomes clear that amid a profusion of minor variations and details there are relatively few major styles. The establishment of a broad, closely-dated typology, a tool that has not previously been available for the study of medieval shoes in Britain, is thus one of the chief aims of the present volume. The breaking down of this typology into subgroups representing individual workshops or phases must remain the task of future generations. In the first chapter, *Shoes from London sites, 1100–1450* (pp. 9–43), the whole period has been divided arbitrarily into seven subperiods, each roughly fifty years – or two generations – long, and the styles current in each

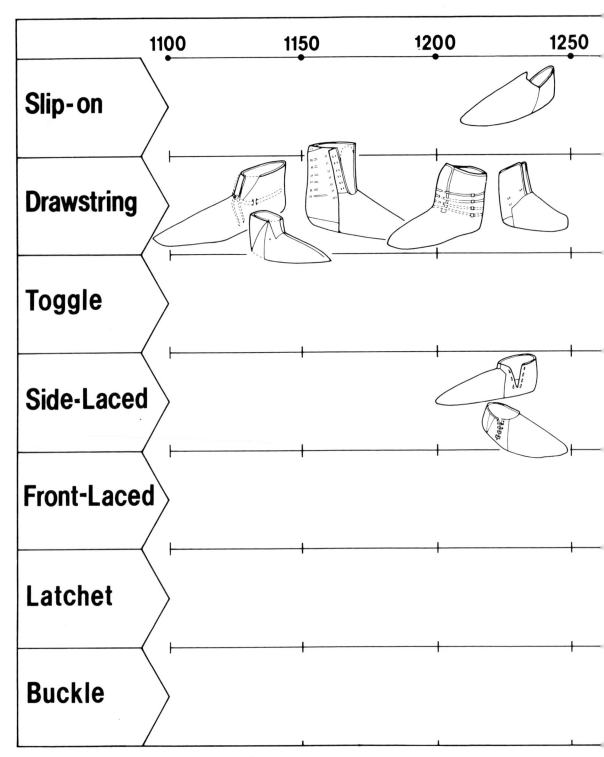

1   Summary of the main types of shoes, ankle-shoes
and boots from London sites, *c*.1100–1450.

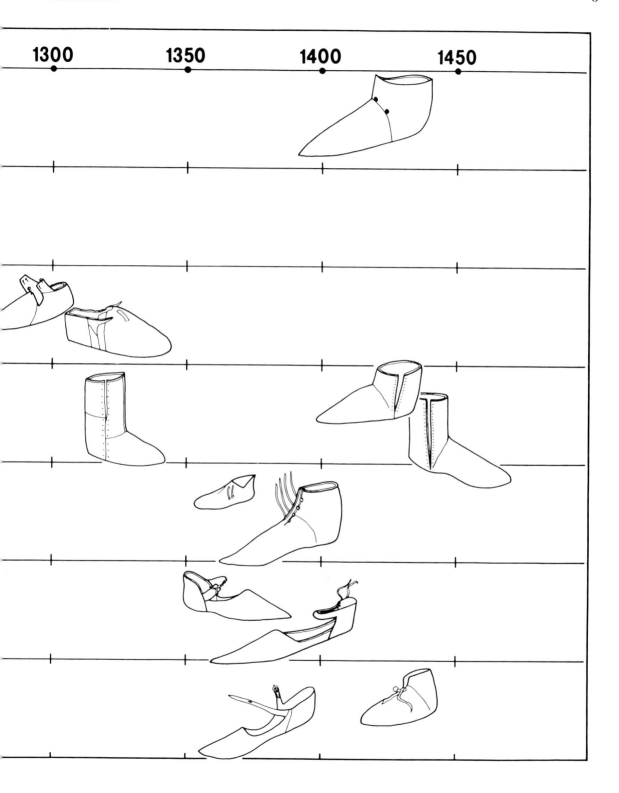

1300 **1350** **1400** **1450**

of these are described. The best surviving
examples are illustrated pictorially, as representatives of their type, and the remainder, which
provide much of the evidence for dating and for the
relative popularity of each style, are normally
summarised in tabular form.

The assessment of what constitutes a 'style' or
'type' is inevitably to some extent subjective, but
for present purposes three main factors have been
taken into account:

(1) the height of the quarters – 'shoes' being
    defined as shoes cut below the ankle, 'ankle-
    shoes' as shoes cut on or just above the ankle,
    and 'boots' as anything higher than these.

(2) the manner of fastening – whether by draw-
    string, toggle, buckle, latchet or lacing (see
    Fig. 1).

(3) the 'cut' – the shape of the toe, for instance,
    or the degree to which the sole is 'waisted'.

From an analysis such as this, the results of
which are summarised in Fig. 1, many groupings
are immediately obvious: the dominance of the
drawstring fastening until the middle of the 13th
century, for example, or the growing importance
of the buckle as a means of fastening shoes from
the mid 14th century onwards. Some trends, such
as the increasing demand for low-cut shoes
through the 14th century – in direct contrast to
the popularity of ankle-shoes and boots both
before and afterwards – must have been almost
imperceptible to those who lived at the time, but
others were much more short-lived, showing that
fashions could change almost as rapidly as they do
today. The latter styles were often the most per-
vasive, dominating the shoe assemblages of their
time. Typical of these are toggle-fastened shoes,
which enjoyed a brief vogue in the late 13th and
early 14th centuries, or curving, pointed toes,
which were popular at the beginning of the 12th
century and again, perhaps for two generations at
most, at the end of the 14th. With the exception of
the side-laced boot, which should perhaps be
regarded as 'working' wear, rather than purely
'fashion' wear, few styles survived for much
longer than a century.

Stylistic changes were often accompanied – and
in some cases made possible – by the technical
developments that are discussed in the second
chapter, *Shoemaking and cobbling* (pp. 44–90).

From this it may be seen, for example, that extremely low-cut shoes, such as were common in
the late 14th century, would have been almost
impossible to manufacture successfully two centuries earlier because the technique of sewing a
strong reinforcement cord along the inside edge to
prevent it from stretching had not yet been
devised. For the citizens of medieval London the
most important developments were probably
those that made shoes more waterproof – first, in
the middle of the 12th century, the invention of a
wedge-shaped strip of leather, the 'rand', which
could be sewn into the lasting-margin to seal the
gap between the sole and the upper and, secondly,
in the first half of the 15th century, the addition of
a complete outer sole to protect the lasting-margin
and upper from direct contact with the ground –
but the modern historian may take more interest in
the observation that after a transitional period in
the late 13th and early 14th centuries shoes
became much more standardised in construction.

Hardly any early shoes are precisely the same
because the difficulty of cutting the upper from a
single piece of leather and, very often, imperfec-
tions in the leather itself made it necessary to use
a number of irregularly-shaped inserts, but many
late 14th- or early 15th-century shoes are identical
and the components virtually interchangeable.
This was partly because the upper was made from
two or three pieces that were smaller and easier
to cut out to a standard pattern and partly, perhaps, because shoemakers now had access to
more regular and reliable supplies of leather.
From this, in turn, it is tempting to go one stage
further and infer a growing sense of organisation
among shoemakers as a profession, with all that
this implies about the imposition of standards,
training, dissemination of techniques and division
of labour between specialists in, say, tanning,
cutting-out or decoration. The Cordwainers'
Company, indeed, had come into being by 1272 if
not earlier, but the loss of most of its records in
the Great Fire precludes any detailed investiga-
tion of its activities at this time.

It was also in the late 14th century that more
sophisticated forms of decoration were introduced, whether in openwork or with delicately
engraved foliate motifs (see below, pp. 79–86),
and, as shown in the following chapter, *Pattens*
(pp. 91–101), that wooden-soled overshoes to
protect the feet in mud or snow first became

at all common. Even so, pattens were still rare in comparison with shoes, and since nearly all late 14th-century examples that have survived were decorated with paint, stitching or embossed motifs it seems that as yet they were worn mainly by the well-to-do. But by the early 15th century the introduction of a new form with a composite leather sole – which may have been worn simply over hose, without any shoe at all – had made this accessory available to everybody.

The history of the patten and of shoemaking techniques thus implies greater sophistication and a more extensive popular 'market' for shoes in late medieval times. A similar conclusion might be drawn from the chapter on *Sizes and wear patterns: social inferences* (pp. 102–111), where it is shown that by the late 14th century children might be provided with shoes as soon as they could walk. In the early 15th century more children's shoes seem to have been made than ever before, and it may be no coincidence that there appeared at this time a form of ankle-shoe, fastened with a buckle or lacing at the front, which would have been more suitable for children's feet than the miniature versions of contemporary adult styles that had normally been worn in the past. But whereas it is possible to identify children's shoes and to estimate the *relative* size of shoes in the collection – relative, that is, to one another in the same archaeological deposit – it is much more difficult to estimate the *original* size, because they may have shrunk and become distorted (see Appendix 2, p. 139 & Table 22). Yet when the figures are adjusted in compensation, it seems likely that medieval feet were generally a little smaller than those of today, though as in modern times they may have suffered from bunions and a range of complaints that were probably aggravated if not caused by the shoes themselves.

Specific wear patterns on an individual shoe are a reminder that archaeology has a natural bias towards the particular rather than the general, and so, in the final chapter, *Shoes in art and literature* (pp. 112–22), an attempt has been made to assess how representative the present collection is of medieval fashions as a whole. From this it emerges that there are several major omissions from the archaeological record, perhaps the most important of which are high boots and buskins. Contemporary illustrations suggest that after *c.*1300 these were worn only by travellers or

huntsmen and so might not be expected from urban sites, but that before that date they were the most common form of footwear; yet none of the 12th- or 13th-century London deposits have yielded boots which rise to more than a third of the height of the knee – and, indeed, these are very rare.

Conversely, there is a strong suspicion that in some cases the illustrations are either 'conventional' or deliberately anachronistic. The embroidered vamp stripe is one of the most easily-recognised forms of decoration, but whereas eleven of the twelve examples in the collection may be dated securely to the 12th century – the twelfth is possibly of the 13th – it continued to be illustrated long into the 14th century, one of the latest appearances being on a brass datable no earlier than 1397. Furthermore, while the comparative ubiquity of archaeological finds would suggest that the vamp stripe conferred no particular status on its wearer, entirely the reverse impression is to be gained from many illustrations. These apparent discrepancies are complicated and not easily resolved, but a possible explanation may be that the vamp stripe originated as a 'luxury' feature – perhaps picked out in gold thread – on the shoes of the well-to-do, which was subsequently copied and mass-produced; meanwhile, iconographically it remained associated with persons of high status and continued to be shown as a convention, long after the shoes themselves had passed out of fashion.

Differences such as these between the archaeological and the illustrative sources are quite frequent, but between the footwear collections from London and elsewhere there is a remarkable similarity. Late 14th-century wooden pattens of precisely the same form and with stamped ornament on the straps were found both at Billingsgate (Fig. 127) and in Coventry (Thomas 1983, Fig. 22); toggle-fastened shoes dominated late 13th- and 14th-century assemblages not only in London but in places as far separated as Kings Lynn (Clarke & Carter 1977, Figs. 164.4, 165.29, 168.73–4) and Sweden (Broberg & Hasselmo 1981, 88–112 & Figs. 83–4); and latchet-fastened shoes with slightly pointed toes from Amsterdam (Baart *et al.* 1977, 74) resemble one of the best-known London styles of the 14th century. That there should be such homogeneity among items so utilitarian as shoes, which presumably were normally made in the towns or villages where they were sold and used, is a further indication of the international character of north-west Europe in medieval times, when the free exchange of ideas at even the humblest level was facilitated by trade, seasonal fairs and overseas travel. In this way, the study of footwear in the present collection can be regarded as a contribution not only to the history of London but to the history of Europe as a whole.

Recording methods, archive and conventions used in the report

As soon as the enormous shoe deposits at 'Baynards Castle' and Trig Lane were exposed it became clear that with the time, finance and manpower available it would not be possible to record and conserve each fragment individually. For this reason it has become the Museum's policy to separate the complete or almost complete shoes and the large fragments with details of fastening, decoration or stitching from the loose soles or clumps, unattached rands and smaller scraps of upper. The former – 'Registered Finds' – are

2 Typical sheet from the full archive catalogue. This section includes part of the early/mid 15th-century group (G15) from Trig Lane (site code: TL 74).

given an individual registration number, unique within each site, and have always been fully conserved; the latter – 'Bulk Finds' – are merely labelled with the number of the archaeological layer – 'context' – in which they were found and, before conservation facilities were expanded in response to the Swan Lane (1981) and Billingsgate (1982) excavations, were simply left to dry out.

In preparation for this volume the bulk finds were recorded only summarily. The number of sole and upper fragments from each context was counted, to give an indication of the size of the original assemblage, and features such as rands, turn-welts, heel-stiffeners or topbands were noted so that their introduction could be dated

```
GROUP 15, c. 1440


Context 274


INDIVIDUALLY REGISTERED


<1249> half

    right foot, adult; oval toe
    sewn, thread surviving
    SOLE:  repaired
    UPPER: parts present: vamp, tongue
           seam position: outside; angled
           fastening method: buckle and strap
    Comments: boot or ankle shoe
              clump only, original sole missing


<1251> half

    boot, right foot, adult; oval toe
    sewn, thread surviving
    SOLE: length 215 mm; one-piece
          worn, repaired
    UPPER: multi-piece
           parts present: vamp, quarters
           seam position: at instep, both sides;
                          horizontal, vertical
           fastening method: side laced


<3441> fragmentary

    Comments: lace hole reinforcement
```

```
UNREGISTERED FRAGMENTS

SOLES:  total numbers: 6 half, 3 fragmentary
        toe shapes: 3 oval
        features: rand; worn; repaired

UPPERS: total numbers: 2 half, 4 fragmentary
        parts present: vamp; quarters
        features: reused

SIZES:  7 adult


Context 275.


INDIVIDUALLY REGISTERED

<1141> half

    boot, left foot, child's; oval toe
    sewn
    SOLE:  length 136 mm; one-piece
           rand
    UPPER: parts present: vamp, quarters, heel
           reinforcement
           seam position: inside

<1142> half

    boot, right foot, child's; rounded toe
    sewn
    SOLE:  length 125 mm; one-piece
    UPPER: one-piece
           parts present: vamp, tongue, quarters
           seam position: inside; vertical
           fastening method: buckle and strap
    Comments: additional ?lace-hole on one side
```

more accurately. But since these fragments are all very small and, being unconserved, have often shrunk abnormally, in practice most of the evidence presented here was taken from the registered finds. Each of these was catalogued in an abbreviated but systematic manner so that the records could be transferred to a computer and lists of, say, all 14th-century front-laced boots or all 12th-century ankle-shoes with vamp stripes could easily be obtained. This made it possible to summarise the contents of each site assemblage and to isolate the best examples for illustration as representatives of their type. Such an approach has been engendered by the sheer size of the collection and the need to publish it economically, but copies of the full catalogues, of both bulk and registered finds sorted by site and archaeological phase (Fig. 2), may be obtained on written application to the Archives Assistant at the Museum of London. The original records and the shoes themselves are permanently stored in the Museum

where, similarly, they may be examined by prior arrangement.

Definitions of nearly all the terms used in this volume may be found in the Glossary (pp. 123–5). All dimensions are in millimetres and the 'length' or 'width' should be regarded as the maximum length or width overall. Except where stated otherwise, the line illustrations are reproduced at a scale of one third. In the graphs of shoe sizes the current 'actual' measurements have been increased by 10 per cent in the case of solvent-dried shoes and 5 per cent for freeze-dried to allow for shrinkage, but as shown below (p. 139) this is a purely nominal average figure. The summary tables of shoe types have been compiled from the registered shoe catalogues, but it should be noted that for the sake of comparability some of the smaller loose fragments – buckle-straps and reinforcement-pieces, in particular – have been omitted when they are not attached to a shoe itself.

Shoes from London sites, 1100–1450

In this chapter shoe fashions in London over a period of 350 years are described. The dating evidence has been provided entirely by archaeology – normally pottery, coins and other datable objects associated with the shoes themselves or dendrochronological dating of timbers associated with the deposits in which they were found – and for full details the reader is referred to Appendix 1 (pp. 131–6). In all cases the illustrations are of actual shoes and boots in the collection, and they are reproduced at a scale of one third. Missing parts are shown with dotted lines where they can be confidently inferred – either from stitching, impressions and other indications on the shoe itself or from similar shoes in the collection where these parts are still present. A letter 'L' or 'R' is used in the illustrations to denote left and right

shoes respectively. Further details, including registration numbers and individual dates, are to be found in the *List of figures and concordance* (pp. 126–30), and 'exploded' drawings of many shoes, showing all the components, can be studied in the following chapter (pp. 51–74).

The early/mid 12th century (Fig. 3)

The earliest shoes to be described in this survey were probably in use during the second quarter of the 12th century and were found in just two deposits, at Seal House and Billingsgate. The groups are very small (8 and 13 registered shoes respectively) but of considerable importance, because they seem to show that there occurred at this time quite a sudden, yet decisive, transition from the styles and techniques of the preceding

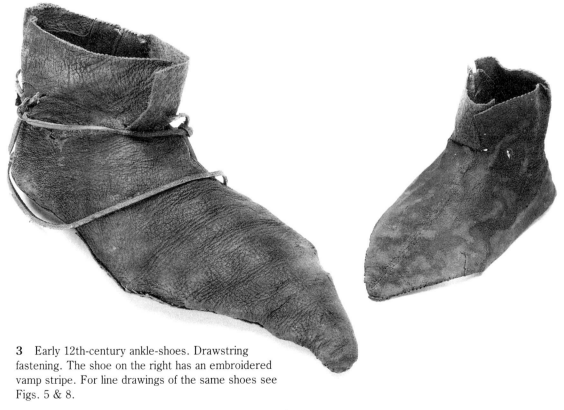

3 Early 12th-century ankle-shoes. Drawstring fastening. The shoe on the right has an embroidered vamp stripe. For line drawings of the same shoes see Figs. 5 & 8.

Saxo-Norman period on the one hand (see Pritchard forthcoming) to those of the later 12th and 13th centuries on the other.

One of the shoes from Billingsgate is an instructive example of a shoe wholly in the Saxo-Norman tradition, incorporating many of the characteristic features of London footwear of the 11th century (Fig. 4). It was almost certainly an ankle-shoe, originally cut just above the ankle bone, and the shape of the sole indicates that it was made to suit a left foot.* It is a turn-shoe (see below, p. 47) and was sewn together – possibly using wool rather than linen thread – with a seam that consists of a normal lasting-margin on the upper and a row of tunnel stitches on the sole, inset slightly from the edge (see also Fig. 82 & p. 51). The sole is straight-sided, as yet without the 'waist' that typifies nearly all later medieval and modern shoes, and has a tapering, pointed heel which rises up at the back and was sewn to an inverted 'V'-shaped cut-out in the quarters. The upper is of 'wrap-around' construction – or 'whole-cut' – with the main seam on the inner side, and directly below the ankle is a group of seven closely bunched slits which examples from earlier deposits suggest would have contained a pair of short interwoven thongs (Pritchard forthcoming). These thongs were presumably ornamental – or at most helped to hold the upper in shape at the quarters – and it is not known how the shoe itself was fastened.

All the other items in the early 12th-century groups differ from this shoe in several important respects. The most obvious is that the soles, although still quite straight-sided, are invariably flat and rounded at the heel. The quarters were sometimes strengthened on the inside with a tri-angular or semicircular reinforcement-piece – 'heel-stiffener' – whose form may in fact have been inspired directly by the earlier 'V'-shaped sole (F. Pritchard, pers. comm.). At the same time, the basic construction of shoes was transformed by discarding the tunnel-stitched seam on the sole in favour of an edge/flesh seam along the edge itself. Rands – wedge-shaped

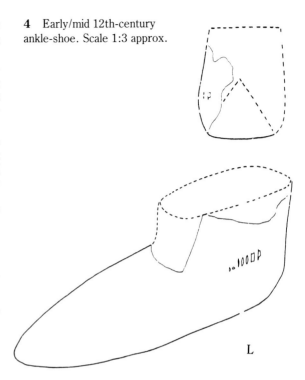

4   Early/mid 12th-century ankle-shoe. Scale 1:3 approx.

strips of leather inserted between the upper and the sole – also appear to have been introduced now in an attempt to make the seam more waterproof, but they did not become common until the end of the 12th century. Only three or four scraps of rands were found in the present deposits – none of these attached to a shoe – and the fact that the lasting-margins normally have very small, closely-spaced stitches (see below, p. 48) is a further indication that in most cases the uppers were still sewn directly to the soles.

Early 12th-century shoes seem either to have been worn as 'slip-ons' or to have been fastened with a leather thong – 'drawstring' – supported in slots cut in the upper and wound once or twice around the quarters. Ankle-shoes, varying in height between those cut straight on the line of the ankle (e.g. Fig. 6) and those rising 1 or 2 inches (25–50 mm) above it (e.g. Figs. 5 & 8), were by far the most popular style. There are only two true shoes (Figs. 7 & 11), and only one boot; this is of a distinctive type to be described in the next section (pp. 14–15 & Figs. 15–16), whereby the drawstring was supported in vertical thongs rather than in cut slots.

---

* All the shoes in the present collection, unlike those from 12th-century Middelburg described by Groenman-van Waateringe (1974, 113–4), can be easily identified as either left or right; similarly, a right-foot boot and a left-foot last are reported from Anglo-Scandinavian York (MacGregor 1982, 138 & Fig. 72 No. 627; 144–5 & Fig. 74).

5 Early/mid 12th-century ankle-shoe. Scale 1:3 approx.

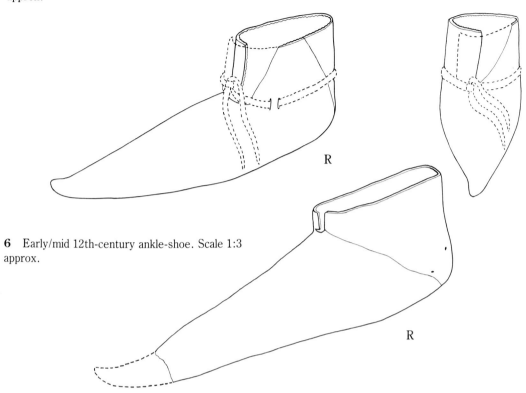

6 Early/mid 12th-century ankle-shoe. Scale 1:3 approx.

Most shoes were pointed at the toe, but rarely can this have been so exaggerated as on two ankle-shoes from Seal House (Figs. 5–6). The toes curve outwards slightly at the tip and may originally have been stuffed to retain their shape, though no evidence for this survives. This was a style which earlier London finds and historical sources show to have originated in the late 11th century (Pritchard forthcoming), but which is found only rarely in deposits post-dating *c*.1150. Both shoes are large, so that they were probably worn by men, and are of similar one-piece construction with a diagonal main seam on the inner side. One is complete but for a small insert at the vamp throat and was fastened by quite a broad drawstring (width of impression, 6 mm) passing through a single row of slots (Fig. 5). As on many shoes of this date (*cf*. Figs. 7, 8) and later, there are the impressions of a binding-stitch on the top edge. From the late 13th century onwards this almost invariably seems to mark the former presence of a leather edging strip, or 'topband', but

for the 12th and early 13th centuries, when very few such topbands have survived, other explanations are possible. It could have been used to secure a fabric or fur lining which is now missing or it may be that the edge was merely bound with thread. The arrangements at the front of the shoe are unclear, but the position of the stitching (Fig. 83) suggests that the missing insert ran right across the instep and may even have overlapped the small flap on the other side. In this way the upper parts of the shoe could be pulled apart, to allow easy insertion of the foot, and then closed to form a snug, double-thickness seal. The second ankle-shoe required no inserts and appears to have been a slip-on type with no additional fastening (Fig. 6). In this case, the absence of stitching (Fig. 84) shows that there was an opening at the vamp throat, and, as on most shoes of this date, the leather has been cut and seamed across the instep to provide flexibility at the point where it bends sharply from the horizontal to the vertical planes.

Many of the features described recur on other shoes of this period, though the toes are only slightly pointed. A large number, however, are decorated with embroidery – normally with a stripe running down the centre of the vamp, but in one instance also with a band on the quarters (see below, pp. 75–9). This is a form of ornament which is first recorded in London deposits of the late 11th century – though elsewhere perhaps earlier – and which appears to have remained popular for about a century, barely outliving the 12th century. Shoes with vamp stripes were made in a range of sizes (the four that are most complete measure *c*.177 (Fig. 8), 185, 225 and 230 mm (Fig. 7), corresponding to the modern sizes 10 (child), 11 (child), 4 (adult) and, probably, 3 (adult) respectively) and, as shown on contemporary illustrations (see below, p. 113), must have been worn by both men and women, though their ubiquity would suggest that their use was not restricted to those of high social status. In comparison with the larger boots and ankle-shoes (cf. Fig. 5), shoes of this kind seem quite lightly made, and it is possible that they were intended mainly for indoor wear.

Only one of the embroidered pieces in the present groups is certainly from a shoe rather than

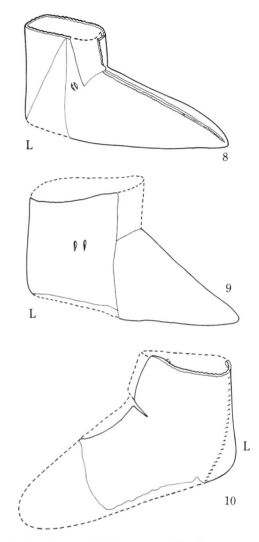

8, 9, 10 Early/mid 12th-century ankle-shoes. Scale: 1:3 approx.

7 Early/mid 12th-century shoe. Scale 1:3 approx.

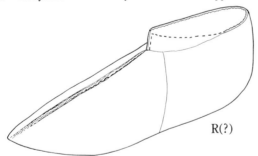

an ankle-shoe (Fig. 7). In many respects it is very similar to the ankle-shoe depicted in Fig. 6, being of essentially one-piece construction – albeit with a small strip insert (now missing) along the upper edge on the inner side – and having a small vertical opening at the instep; it was apparently worn as a slip-on. The remainder are all ankle-shoes fastened with drawstrings which pass through a single, or in one case a double, row of slots – usually one slot on either side of the instep. The illustrated example (Fig. 8) has a stripe made up of

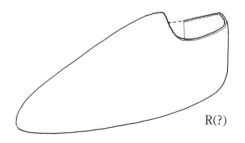

11 Early/mid 12th-century shoe. Scale: 1:3 approx.

three rows of embroidery, rather than a single row as on the shoe, and seems originally to have had a large triangular insert on the inner side; there was a second insert at the instep, and the arrangements here may have been similar to those on the long pointed ankle-shoe (*cf.* Figs. 5 & 86), including a long flap which overlapped the small existing flap on the outer side.

The plain shoes of this date can be summarised briefly, because few merit particular attention. All were made by the 'wrap-around' method, but one is slightly different in that it was designed to include a small triangular insert (now missing) in the angle between the main seam and the lasting margin on the inner side (Fig. 9). This is the first appearance of a cutting style which occurred sporadically throughout the later 12th century but became standard only in the early 13th. Some other ankle-shoes are noteworthy for the presence of large cut-outs in the upper. These would have had an ornamental value, contrasting the colours and texture of the leather with those of the wearer's hose beneath. One (not illustrated) had a single circular cut-out in the quarters, which was seamed at the edge, either to prevent it from stretching or, possibly, to secure a lining. Another (Fig. 10), which is additionally unusual in that it seems to have had a large triangular reinforcement-piece on the *outside* of the quarters, is cut very low over the toes in the manner of a modern 'court' or 'bar' shoe, a style which is occasionally seen on contemporary illustrations (see below, pp. 113–4).

The final shoe to be discussed is quite different from any other in these groups, because the upper appears to have been made entirely from a single piece of leather and was shaped at both the heel and vamp throat (Fig. 11). There is nothing to suggest that it was fastened by a drawstring or any other means, and its function may have been that of a modern slipper. The style evidently had a long life, for several examples were found in deposits of a century later (see below, pp. 16–17 and Figs. 18–19).

The later 12th century

Fashions in the second half of the 12th century are represented by three groups of rather fragmentary shoes: one from Milk Street (3 registered shoes), a second from Seal House (10 registered shoes) and a third from Billingsgate (28 registered shoes). As in the first half of the century, all the uppers are of one-piece 'wrap around' construction, but most of the soles – some of which were made in two sections – are now clearly waisted in the centre. At the same time, the exaggerated toes of the earlier period passed completely out of fashion – there is only one possible example – and while some shoes, especially those in the older tradition with embroidered vamps (see below), still retained slight points (*cf.* Fig. 12), most now had toes that were quite broad and rounded (Figs. 13, 16). The front of one such shoe survives almost intact, and, significantly, it has a rand still stitched between the upper and the sole. Unattached rands, rare in the early 12th-century groups, were found in considerable quantities at Seal House, suggesting that they had come into use almost universally by the late 12th century.

Drawstrings continued to be by far the most common means of fastening – which makes their absence from contemporary illustrations (see below, p. 114) all the more surprising – but there are also two fragments from tall ankle-shoes or boots which were laced at the side. This fastening method was to become popular in the first half of the next century (see below, p. 18), and remained in use thereafter until the very end of the medieval period. Among the drawstring shoes themselves, at least one early 12th-century style lasted into the second half of the century. This was the ankle-shoe, sometimes with an embroidered stripe on the vamp, fastened by a drawstring which passed through a single, or more rarely a double, row of slots (*cf.* Fig. 8). There are at least four examples from Billingsgate, one from Seal House and two from Milk Street. As before they tend to be in the smaller sizes, and the illustrated example (Fig. 12) must have been worn by a very young child. It is complete except for an insert on the inner side, which would originally have extended across the instep and sealed the vamp throat by joining the small surviving flap on the outer side.

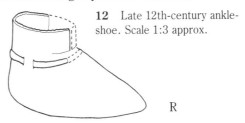

12 Late 12th-century ankle-shoe. Scale 1:3 approx.

R

In the same deposits, however, are at least twelve fragments of a rather different style, a tall ankle-shoe or full boot. The most complete (Fig. 13) is a man's boot, very rounded at the toe, which originally stood to a height of *c.*200 mm and thus reached nearly to mid calf. It is of 'wrap-around' construction with a small triangular insert at the base on the inner side – common to many ankle-shoes and boots of this period – and two more inserts at the top and above the instep. There was no stitching along the upper edge, for binding or a topband, but there were reinforcement-pieces over the opening flaps at the front; and, since stitching runs right across the instep, almost certainly there was a tongue, though this itself has not survived and its form is uncertain. The boot has four sets of thong slots, arranged in seven tiers, and there are impressions from a narrow draw-string, *c.*1 mm wide, running horizontally between them; it is not clear, however, from the surviving fragments whether this was a single string wound continuously round the leg or seven separate strings tied together at the front. On a second, smaller and much more fragmentary boot of the same general type part of the drawstring remains in place (Fig. 14). There are three tiers of slots surviving and the string, which appears to have been deliberately twisted, perhaps for decorative effect, is knotted at the lowest slot on the outer side; this suggests that it was then wound continuously upwards in concentric circles around the ankle.

On the examples already described the draw-strings passed through slots cut in the upper, but some boots had a more complex and ornamental arrangement whereby they passed through loops in thongs *c.*5 mm broad, which ran vertically upwards. These thongs were themselves threaded loosely through pairs of slots, and each had a spade-shaped terminal which was anchored against the lowest slot on the inside. The most complete boot of this type comes from a deposit of the 13th century but is best considered here in the general discussion of the style (Fig. 15). It is of normal 'wrap-around' construction, with a trapezoidal insert on the inner side, a topband and a long triangular edging strip which was sewn to the vamp throat at the base and formed an overlapping flap for opening. The boot has only one vertical thong – on the outer side over the ankle, where it could be seen to best effect – and three series of

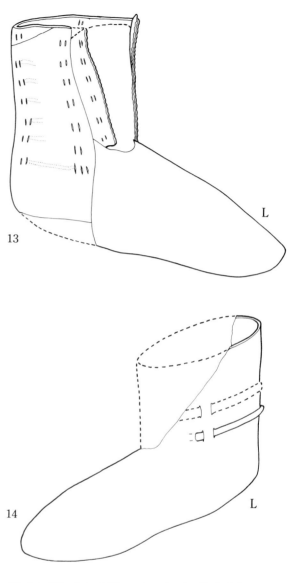

13, 14, 15 Late 12th-century boots. Scale 1:3 approx.

slots, at the instep, on the inner side and at the heel, to support the drawstring. The string itself is only partly in place, but it seems possible that it was secured by a knot tied against the inside of the single perforation at the instep and then wound continuously upwards through the slots and thong. The purpose of the small surviving knot in the other end of the drawstring is unclear.

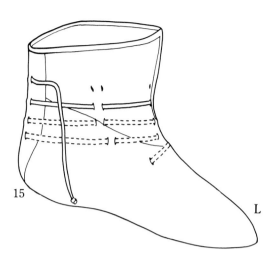

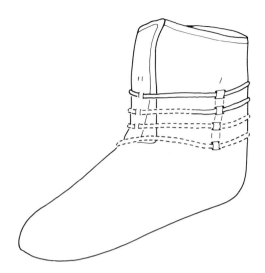

Other examples of this type had more than one vertical thong. The most complete of these has three remaining, one on either side and the third in the middle of the instep (Fig. 16). It is an ankle-shoe and probably survives to its original height, although even this is not certain because it has been extensively repaired both on the sole and upper, and subsequently cut up for reuse; the quarters are almost entirely lost. There seems to have been an opening at the instep – though it is not known if the sides overlapped – and, since one of the side thongs has four loops but the central thong only three, it is likely that this boot also was laced continuously with a single drawstring.

The early/mid 13th century (Fig. 17)

It is to the first half of the 13th century that the earliest substantial assemblages from the London waterfront belong. Important groups were found at Seal House (two successive deposits containing 21 and 9 registered shoes respectively) and Billingsgate (three deposits, 8, 6, and 24 registered shoes). These are summarised in Tables 1–2, where it should be noted that the groups from each site have been amalgamated, since they are too small to support individual statistical analysis and, in any case, show little perceptible difference in the types represented.

It is immediately obvious that the Seal House and Billingsgate assemblages are very similar (Tables 1–2). The ratio of shoes:ankle-shoes:boots is similar, and the same range of

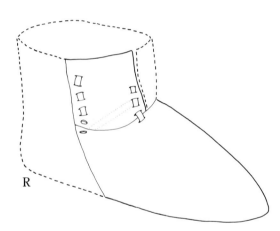

16   Late 12th-century ankle-shoe. Scale 1:3 approx.

fastening types is represented in almost identical proportions. Nearly all the shoes appear to have been assembled with rands, and the soles have quite a pronounced waisted shape, generally with a round or oval-shaped toe (see, for example, Figs. 21, 24). As was invariably the practice in the 12th century, the uppers are mostly of one-piece 'wrap-around' construction, with inserts added where necessary, but there are for the first time several examples of shoes made in two main sections – vamp and quarters – with seams on both sides of the foot (Figs. 25, 28). This is a type of construction found sporadically throughout the later 13th and 14th centuries but which did not

17 Early/mid 13th-century boot and ankle-shoes. The boot was fastened with a drawstring but the three ankle-shoes were laced at the side. For line drawings of the same shoes see Figs. 25, 15, 27 & 28.

become widespread until the second half of the 14th century (see below, pp. 32–3). Decoration is very rare, now that embroidered shoes had passed out of fashion, though it should not be forgotten that the concentric lacing circles on tall ankle-shoes and boots may have had some ornamental, as well as functional, value.

Ankle-shoes or boots are by far the most common form of footwear, accounting for over half the total number of individually registered finds (Tables 1–2). There are just six shoes cut below the ankle, and three of these may have been a special type of indoor slipper similar to that found in one of the early 12th-century groups (Figs. 18–19; cf. Fig. 11 and p. 13). The two which are most complete were both made from single pieces of very thin, soft leather, with a finely stitched butt seam joining the sole to the upper, almost certainly without rands. There was binding or a top-band (not surviving) but no trace of any fastening. One (Fig. 18) is conventionally styled, high at the instep, whereas the other (Fig. 19) is cut very low

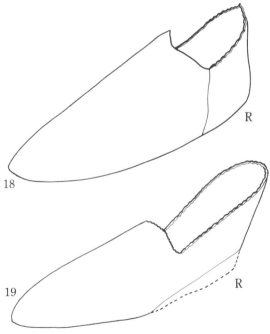

18, 19 Early/mid 13th-century shoes. Scale 1:3 approx.

Table 1. Shoes (all sizes) from Seal House, early/mid 13th century.

	Drawstring				Buckle	Toggle	Slip-on	Side-laced	Not known	Total
	Type 1	Type 2	Type 3	Uncertain type						
Shoe	—	—	—	—	—	—	2	1	—	3
Ankle-shoe	3	—	—	—	1	2	—	2	—	8
Boot	2	5	1	1	—	—	—	—	—	9
Not known	2	—	—	2	—	—	—	—	6	10
Total	7	5	1	3	1	2	2	3	6	30

Drawstring

Type 1

Type 2

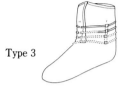
Type 3

Table 2: Shoes (all sizes) from Billingsgate, early/mid 13th century.

	Drawstring				Toggle	Slip-on	Side-laced	Not known	Total
	Type 1	Type 2	Type 3	Uncertain type					
Shoe	—	—	—	—	—	1	2	—	3
Ankle-shoe	6	—	—	—	2	—	—	—	8
Boot	2	4	4	1	—	—	—	—	11
Not known	—	2	2	3	—	—	1	8	16
Total	8	6	6	4	2	1	3	8	38

over the toes but is high at the heel; it is also unusual in that it has a long strip insert around the lower part of the quarters, possibly designed for easy replacement in the event of severe wear to the heel.

As in the 12th century the most common style was the low boot or ankle-shoe fastened with a drawstring wound once or twice around the leg, normally just below the ankle (Tables 1–2; Figs. 20–23). Impressions and the size of the slots show that the string was often quite broad, measuring up to *c.*5 mm across. The 13th-century examples tend to rise much higher up the leg than their 12th-century predecessors and to be roomier and more rounded at the toe, but again their appearance almost exclusively in the smaller sizes reinforces the impression that this was a style favoured mainly by women and children. On the other hand, the full boots and side-laced shoes (described below) almost all seem to have been worn by men.

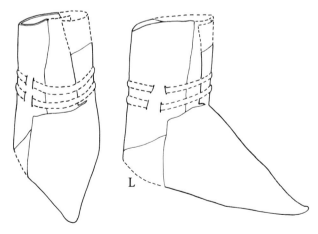

20 Early/mid 13th-century ankle-shoe. Scale 1:3 approx.

As far as can be judged from the surviving fragments, nearly all the low boots and ankle-shoes
shared a similar one-piece 'wrap-around' type of
construction with a main seam on the inner side
and, normally, a small triangular insert at the base
(Figs. 20, 21, 23). The latter is a detail found only
rarely before the early 13th century. A further
difference from earlier examples is the absence of
an insert at the vamp throat such as could provide
an overlapping flap opening (*cf.* Figs. 5, 8). Instead, the sides normally meet roughly in the
centre and, since there is no trace of a tongue, it
seems that the front of the boot would have been
closed tightly over the instep by the drawstring
but may have remained open at the top. This
difference can be appreciated by comparing the
example illustrated in Fig. 20, which was made
entirely in the 12th-century manner and even has
a pointed toe, with those in Figs. 21–23.
Topbands and other reinforcement-pieces are not
common but, occasionally, as on the very small
child's shoe illustrated (Fig. 23), the presence of a
butt seam along the upper edge suggests that an
upper section may have been added to form quite
a tall boot.

The full boot fastened with a drawstring wound
many times round the leg is a further style which
continued in use into the early 13th century. The
elaborate type, in which the string passed through
separate vertical thongs (*cf.* Figs. 15–16), is
represented only twice, but there are several
examples of the simple version. The illustrated
boot (Fig. 24) is very similar to one found in the
earlier groups (Fig. 13) – even to the extent of
having the same strip insert along the upper edge
– but, like several others of this date, it has
circular holes, rather than slits, for a very thin
string less than 2 mm across. It is also remarkable
for the number and complexity of the inserts on
the inner side, a feature shared with one of the
ankle-shoes described below (Fig. 27) and
perhaps suggestive of difficulties in obtaining hides
of sufficient size and quality at this time (see
further, p. 46).

Among the most interesting shoes of this period
are those laced at the side. This style of fastening has hardly been found in earlier London
assemblages and, conversely, has been found only
sporadically in later ones before emerging as the
'standard' in the early/mid 15th century (see
below, p. 43). There are six examples in all, of

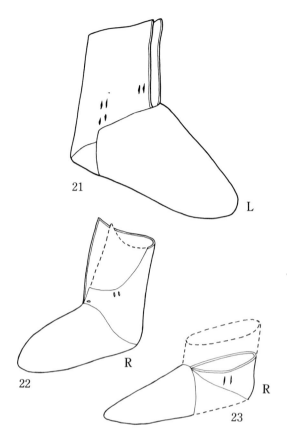

21, 22, 23 Early/mid 13th-century ankle-shoes.
Scale 1:3 approx.

which three are shoes cut below the ankle and two
are ankle-shoes (Tables 1–2). All seem to have
been laced on the inner side. Among the shoes,
the two which are most complete are almost identical in form, being quite high at the instep but very
low at the heel; both may originally have had topbands (*cf.* Figs. 27 & 90) – though these no longer
survive – and reinforcement-pieces over the lace-
holes on the inside. One (Fig. 25) has elaborate
openwork decoration based on lunate, circular,
rectangular and cruciform motifs, and is of two-
part construction; the vamp and quarters remain
intact but a small insert, which joined the vamp on
the inner side and carried one set of lace-holes, is
now missing. The other shoe (Fig. 26) is made
entirely in one piece, and on the vamp throat is a
rough knife cut with a pair of holes on either side,
which possibly was made by the wearer to relieve
pressure on a high instep.

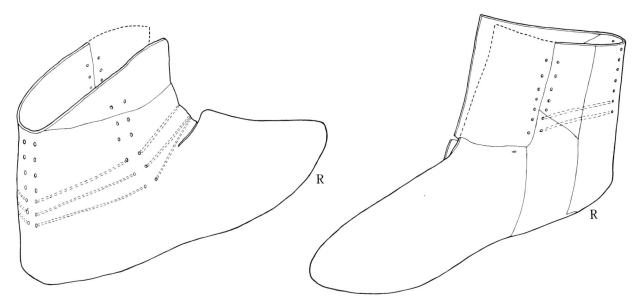

24 Early/mid 13th-century boot. Scale 1:3 approx.
25, 26 Early/mid 13th-century shoes. Scale 1:3 approx.

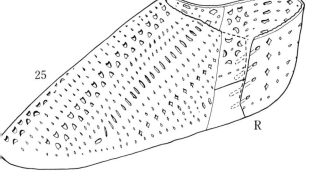

One of the ankle-shoes, although taller, is very similar in general appearance to the shoes, but the inner side is an extraordinary patchwork of at least three separate inserts (Fig. 27); one large piece contains nine lace-holes, a second tiny fragment connects it to the heel and contains just a single lace-hole, and a third (missing) strip perhaps ran along the top edge to form a flap opening similar to those seen on some 12th-century shoes (*cf.* Fig. 7). In this case the lace itself remains in position. It was knotted behind one of the bottom holes, was threaded upwards and, presumably, was knotted at the very top, an arrangement that hardly can have

27 Early/mid 13th-century ankle-shoe. Scale 1:3 approx.

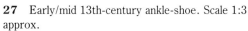

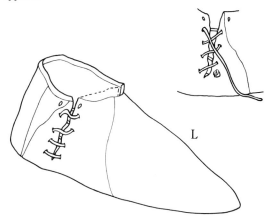

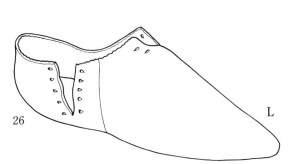

held the shoe very tightly on the foot. The second complete ankle-shoe is radically different in construction, since the vamp and quarters are separate units joined by identical seams in the same position on both sides of the foot (Fig. 28). There was a topband, a heel-stiffener and a reinforcement-piece over the lace-holes, which are large and triangular. The holes are uneven in number (three on one side, four on the other) and seem to have been at least partly decorative, for impressions show that they have been pulled out of shape by a small round lace rather than a broad thong – probably a single lace threaded upwards in the manner illustrated in Fig. 27.

The few remaining shoes in this group are all of types discussed elsewhere and merit only brief individual attention. One is a small ankle-shoe, originally fastened with a buckle, but in general

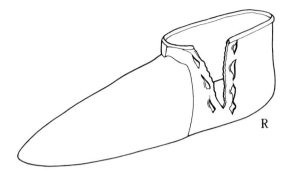

28 Early/mid 13th-century ankle-shoe. Scale 1:3 approx.

Table 3. Shoes (all sizes) from Swan Lane, late 13th century.

| | Toggle | | | | | | |
	Type 1	Type 2	Type 3	Uncertain type	Drawstring	Not known	Total
Shoe	6	—	—	—	—	1	7
Ankle-shoe	5	4	—	—	—	2	11
Boot	—	—	3	1	—	—	4
Not known	5	2	—	7	—	4	18
Total	16	6	3	8	—	7	40

Table 4. Shoes (all sizes) from Ludgate, early 14th century.

| | Toggle | | | | | | |
	Type 1	Type 2	Type 3	Uncertain type	Drawstring	Not known	Total
Shoe	1	2	—	—	—	—	3
Ankle-shoe	—	2	—	1	3	—	6
Boot	—	—	1	—	1	—	2
Not known	1	1	—	6	3	4	15
Total	2	5	1	7	7	4	26

Toggle

Type 1

Type 2

Type 3

appearance and construction it is remarkably similar to a common early 15th-century type (*cf.*, for example, Fig. 63) and almost certainly should be considered intrusive. The others are all parts of ankle-shoes with a toggle fastening, a totally new style which seems to have originated in the early 13th century and became increasingly fashionable in its second half. The most complete of these shoes has accordingly been reserved for detailed description below (Fig. 33).

The late 13th and early 14th centuries

It is these years which mark decisively the transition from the styles of the early medieval period – in particular, the drawstring fastening – to those of the late medieval. Groups from four sites, Swan Lane (40 registered shoes; Table 3), Billingsgate (16 shoes), Trig Lane (17 shoes) and Ludgate (26 shoes: Table 4), illustrate these developments.

On shoes of all kinds the round or oval toe shape which developed in the first half of the 13th century remained in vogue, though occasionally a rather more pointed style is seen (*cf.*, for example, Fig. 31). The full boot continued to be produced, but it seems that the low boot or tall ankle-shoe, which was so popular earlier, steadily declined in numbers, in favour of the low ankle-shoe or shoe. This fact is not immediately obvious when comparing Tables 3–4 with Tables 1–2, but it should be remembered that the ankle-shoes counted in the former are almost all of the 'low', toggle-fastened type illustrated in Figs. 32–3, whereas those in the latter are mainly of the 'tall', drawstring type described above (pp. 17–18 & Figs. 20–23).

There was one major innovation in manufacturing technique in the second half of the 13th century: the use of a stout cord stitched just inside a cut edge to reinforce opening flaps and other areas of potential weakness (see further, pp. 22, 51). Almost without exception, shoes of all kinds had uppers made as before in one piece, normally with a main seam on the inner side, but it appears that now there was much greater uniformity in styling and construction – made possible, in particular, by the avoidance of irregularly-shaped inserts at the sides and instep – and that the leather used was more regular in thickness and texture. This coincided with a greater use of calfskin for uppers, rather than sheep- or goat-skin as in the 12th and early 13th centuries, and it

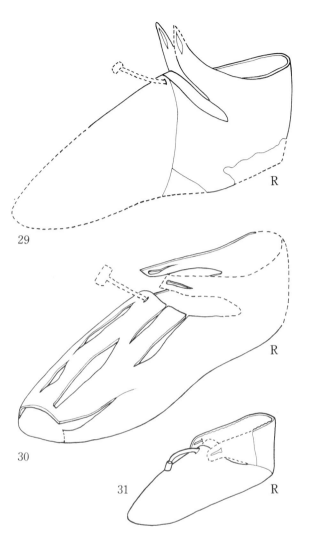

29, 30, 31 Late 13th-century shoes. Scale 1:3 approx.

may be that the supplies of livestock to the London market were reorganised considerably at this time (see below, pp. 44–6).

As Tables 3 and 4 show, fashions in the late 13th and early 14th centuries were dominated by the toggle fastening (Figs. 29–34). It is remarkable that this was the only type of fastening definitely recorded at Swan Lane, accounting for 28 of the 33 registered shoes, and the figures for Billingsgate are broadly comparable (9 shoes with toggles and just 4 certainly fastened in another way). At

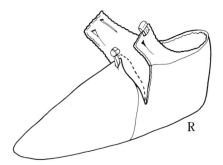

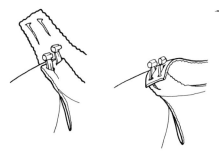

32   Late 13th-century ankle-shoe. Scale 1:3 approx.

Ludgate and, probably, Trig Lane there is a greater range of fastenings, but toggles still account for well over half the types recorded. They were used on boots and shoes made in a variety of styles. The simplest, invariably a shoe or ankle-shoe cut below or on the line of the ankle, has a pair of identical flaps, each with a 'button-hole' for fastening to a single toggle in the centre of the vamp throat. The first illustrated example (Fig. 29) is made entirely in one piece – though very often (*cf.* Fig. 31 and Fig. 36 from a subsequent group) one of the flaps was made as a separate insert – and there is a long semicircular tongue which runs right across the vamp throat to provide flexibility over the instep while at the same time covering the open areas behind the flaps. The front of the shoe is almost completely lost, and originally there was a topband stitched to all the upper edges except the tongue. The toggle, also now missing, would have been formed from a leather lace whose end was rolled back on itself, passed through a slit and pulled tight; the other end was then threaded through the perforation in the vamp throat and stitched down on the underside.

On at least one shoe of this type the vamp has been slashed through with a knife. The toe of the illustrated example has been sliced off and the slashes, which take the form of elongated lozenges, seem originally to have been arranged roughly in two bands across the foot (Fig. 30). This was probably done for decorative or practical purposes, to create a form of open sandal, but it might possibly be compared with the process of ritual defacement whereby shoes are placed as a good-luck offering in the chimney or attic of a new building. In her discussion of a similarly-slashed 15th-century shoe from the Austin Friars, Leicester, Clare Allin (Mellor & Pearce 1981,

155; following Swann) has traced this practice – well attested in early modern times – back into the 17th century but not definitely into the medieval period.

Ankle-shoes rising slightly higher over the ankle were normally provided with two or three toggles (Figs. 32–3). They were very similar in style and construction to the shoes already described, except that on the inner side was an insert which carried a single 'buttonhole' and either one or two toggles passing through slots and stitched down on the inside. To close the shoe, the flaps were first secured independently to the toggle on the vamp and then were 'buttoned' together to protect the higher parts of the instep (Fig. 32). In some cases the edges of the flaps were strengthened with a cord; normally this ran along the inside surface and was held in place by a second, finer thread stitched across it (see further p. 51 and Fig. 81), but on one of the illustrated examples (Fig. 33) it seems that the cord itself was stitched through the leather, because there is a row of short but broad stitch impressions running in the same direction as the 'buttonholes'.

33   Mid 13th-century ankle-shoe. Scale 1:3 approx.

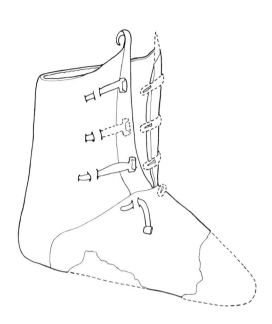

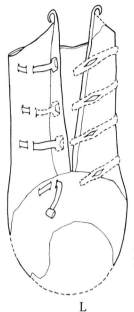

34 Late 13th-century boot. Scale 1:3 approx.

L

Full boots were also fastened with toggles but here they were seated in a series of slots spaced evenly up the inner side; on the outer side was a corresponding set of slotted tags which were secured over the toggles at the front of the boot. The most complete example of this type (Fig. 34) is of 'wrap-around' construction with an insert extending to the full height at the front. It appears to have had no tongue, but where they meet at the instep the sides were edged with long strips, one of which rose above the top of the boot and curled over in a decorative flourish; this feature can be seen – albeit in much less exaggerated fashion – on a boot from an earlier deposit (Fig. 13) and may have been restricted to boots of this general form and dimensions.

The popularity of the toggle fastening is to some extent surprising, not least because it seems to have been impossible to adjust the length of the toggle tags to fit the individual foot. In most cases where it survives the tag is so long that the flaps cannot have closed tightly over the instep and walking would have been very difficult. Indeed, as a means of fastening shoes the toggle has a curiously intermittent history, at least in London, for it first appears on a late Saxon ankle-shoe in the pre-1974 Museum collection (Pritchard forthcoming; *cf.* MacGregor 1982, Fig. 72 No. 627 for

an example from Anglo-Scandinavian York). Here it is to be seen low down on the outer side, securing a broad flap passing right across the instep. Yet its revival in the late 13th century, after a lapse of at least 200 years, was of considerable significance in the development of medieval shoe fashion because it introduced the concept of fastening a shoe across the instep by means of two movable flaps – a concept which was standardised in the buckles and straps of the late 14th century. This in turn made possible the making of low-cut shoes which, because of the shape of the foot, are inherently unsuited to fastening with a drawstring or with laces at the side. Toggle-fastened shoes and ankle-shoes appear to have been made in a range of sizes, including those suitable for very young children. The smallest in the collection (Fig. 31) is an exact replica of an adult shoe, but now lacks its tongue and topband; an insert which carried the second 'buttonhole' is also missing from the inner side. Another shoe is only slightly larger, having a sole which measures just 169 mm. When allowance is made for 5 per cent shrinkage during conservation, this would correspond to the modern child's size 8. The other three complete soles measure between 240 and 246 mm (modern adult's size 4–5).

The only other style which was at all common in

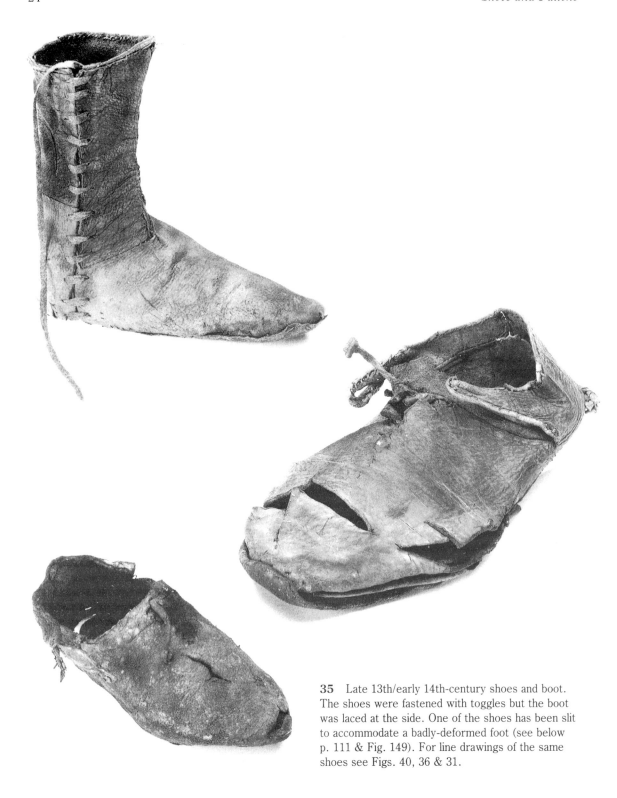

35 Late 13th/early 14th-century shoes and boot. The shoes were fastened with toggles but the boot was laced at the side. One of the shoes has been slit to accommodate a badly-deformed foot (see below p. 111 & Fig. 149). For line drawings of the same shoes see Figs. 40, 36 & 31.

Table 5. Shoes (all sizes) from 'Baynards Castle', early/mid 14th century.

| | Toggle | | | | | | | | | |
	Type 1	Type 2	Uncertain type	Buckle	Latchet	Buckle or latchet	Side-laced	Front-laced	Not known	Total
Shoe	11	—	—	1	1	1	1	2	3	20
Ankle-shoe	—	1	—	—	—	—	—	—	—	1
Boot	—	—	—	—	—	—	6	—	1	7
Not known	1	—	1	—	1	—	3	—	7	13
Total	12	1	1	1	2	1	10	2	11	41

Toggle

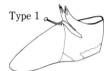

the late 13th and early 14th centuries was the ankle-shoe or boot fastened with a drawstring. Examples of this date are very similar in appearance and construction to those made in the early 13th century (*cf.* Figs. 20–23), but it seems that now they were mainly worn by very small children, for whom perhaps toggles were considered as yet unmanageable. The only ankle-shoe of this type from Billingsgate measures no more than *c.* 120 mm, and three of those from Ludgate (Table 4) are of similar dimensions. The Ludgate group, however, also contains several quite large adult boots or ankle-shoes with drawstring fastenings; it is possible that these were very old when they were lost or, alternatively and more plausibly, that since the site lies in the extreme west of the City, far removed from Swan Lane and Billingsgate in the south-east, the incidence of different styles varied slightly from one place to another, in accordance with the demands and occupations of the local inhabitants.

The mid 14th century (Fig. 35)
This period is poorly represented by finds from London. There is only one large group, from 'Baynards Castle', but fortunately it is exceptionally well preserved (41 individually registered shoes). The other groups are smaller and more scrappy, though since they come from three quite widely separated sites can be expected to provide useful evidence to confirm the main trends. One is

from Trig Lane (6 registered shoes), the second is from Dowgate (9 registered shoes) and the third is from Custom House (4 registered shoes).

The 'Baynards Castle' assemblage is of especial interest, because it shows a further stage in the development of the trends first distinguished in the late 13th century – in particular, the clear polarisation between, on the one hand, below-the-ankle shoes, which account for about half the total, and, on the other, full boots rising to nearly mid-calf height, which account for a fifth (see Table 5). Low boots terminating just above the ankle, so common in the early 13th century, are hardly present at all. Both boots and shoes seem to have been made in a similar range of sizes – the six shoes with complete soles vary from 180 to 245 mm in length, and the four complete boots from 172 to 240 mm – and this could suggest that they were worn equally by men and women, but that they had rather different functions. Boots of this height would be suitable for work and outdoor occupations, whereas the shoes might be more appropriate for indoor use.

It is clear that by this date styles and constructional methods had become further standardised – again in continuation of a late 13th-century trend – and that individual examples show much less variation than their 12th- and early 13th-century predecessors. Nearly all the shoes were fastened with toggles and the boots were all laced at the side. Boots with toggle fastenings of the type which was popular in the late 13th century seem to have been worn no longer, except by very small children (*cf.* Fig. 38), and drawstrings seem to have disappeared completely.

These inferences from the 'Baynards Castle' assemblage are broadly confirmed by the groups from the other three sites, although the distinction

36, 37 Early/mid 14th-century
shoes. Scale 1:3 approx.

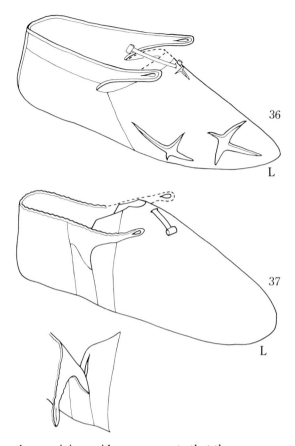

between toggle-fastening for shoes and side-lacing for boots is not so precise: from both Custom House and Dowgate, for example, there are fragmentary remains of side-laced shoes as well as boots. But at all three sites, as at 'Baynards Castle', the basic forms are similar. Most uppers continued to share the 'wrap-around' method of construction, with a main seam on the inner side, and from the soles it is clear that the oval toe shape returned to fashion after the brief vogue of a more pointed style at the end of the 13th century; some of the toggle-fastened shoes, in particular, have soles with broad, rounded toes but quite pronounced 'waists' at the centre.

Table 5 shows that, at 'Baynards Castle' at least, nearly all the toggle-fastened shoes are of the type with a single toggle at the instep and a single 'buttonhole' on the flap at each side; the more elaborate version, with additional toggles on one of the flaps, had evidently passed almost completely out of fashion by this date. The shoes are mostly very similar in construction and appearance to those of the late 13th century, but one of the illustrated examples (Fig. 36) is unusual in that the inner side is made up of two inserts, set one above the other with a seam at the heel. A topband ran along the upper edges and was made in two parts: the section at the rear, behind the flaps, is of thin leather, folded double to give a smooth edge, whereas the front section is of stout, single-thickness leather which offered a much rougher finish, indistinguishable from the material of the upper itself. This shoe was apparently much used by its owner, for a repair piece was stitched to the sole and subsequently worn through, and three major groups of incisions were made in the vamp, presumably to make room for toes that had become badly swollen or deformed (see below, pp. 110–11).

A significant development in the design of toggle-fastened shoes is shown by two examples from Dowgate and two from 'Baynards Castle'. The most complete of these is illustrated (Fig. 37). Only the inner side is wholly preserved, but

the surviving evidence suggests that the arrangements on both sides of the shoe were very similar. The inner side itself contains an inserted section made up of three small pieces of leather, one of which has a 'buttonhole', cut and stitched together in such a way that the largest piece lies partly behind the other two (Fig. 37; *cf.* Fig. 95). The purpose of this was to provide a watertight seal behind a movable 'buttonhole' flap, and it enabled the flap itself to be transferred from the top edge of the shoe to a position lower down the side. This in turn would probably have provided a much tighter and more comfortable fit, since the flaps would have acted as a continuous band, extending from the arch of the foot and right across the instep.

There is only one shoe suitable for a very small child. It measures just 109 mm at the sole, equivalent to the modern child's size 2 (allowing for shrinkage by 10 per cent), and is a low boot that differs in several important respects from the

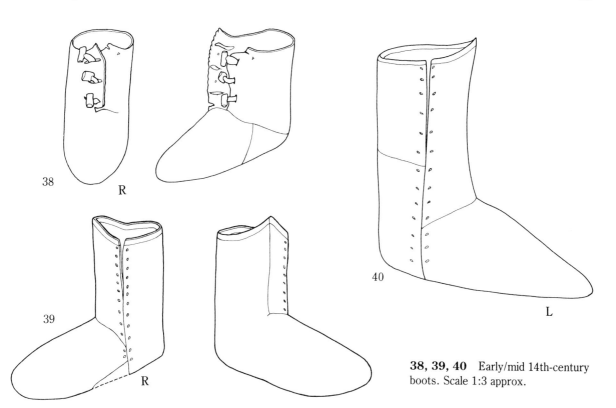

38, 39, 40 Early/mid 14th-century boots. Scale 1:3 approx.

styles normally worn by adults (Fig. 38). In construction it resembles an early 13th-century drawstring ankle-shoe, having a horizontal seam on the instep and a triangular insert near the base on the inner side (*cf.* Figs. 21 & 23), but it was fastened by three toggles. The 'buttonholes' are cut directly in the flap on the outer side, rather than being on separate tags, and the edge of the flap was reinforced either with an applied band or, more probably, with plain stitching.

The side-laced boots are all of similar relative height and are very standardised in construction. They are roughly as tall as they are long, and probably reached about a third of the distance to the knee (Figs. 39–40). The uppers were invariably of 'wrap-around' type (*cf.* Fig. 97), and on the inner side there was a very short main seam running from the sole to the bottom pair of lace-holes; this seam, which held the whole boot in shape, must always have been a potential point of weakness, and severe damage can often be seen here (Figs. 39–40). The only additional piece was normally a long rectangular insert which extended the full

height from the instep; the horizontal seam which joined it to the vamp would have provided flexibility at an abrupt change of angle, since most boots of this type seem to have fitted the foot quite closely, and the straight vertical seam may have given a rather angular appearance over the shin – especially since the boot was generally a little taller at the front than at the back. On very large boots a strip was often used to raise the top edge, just as on boots of the 12th and 13th centuries (*cf.* Fig. 13), and on one example there is an entire upper section which encircled the quarters and heightened the boot by as much as 80 mm (Fig. 40). Topbands seem to have been provided invariably, and the surviving examples are thin strips of leather folded double over the edge. The lace-holes were reinforced with leather facings on the inside (*cf.* Fig. 97), but there were no tongues, even though the holes reached almost to the ground; regrettably, the laces themselves have not remained in place on any of the boots in the present groups.

The 'Baynards Castle' assemblage contains

41 Late 14th-century ankle-shoe and shoes. The children's shoes were laced at the front, but the adults' shoes were fastened with either a latchet or a buckle. For line drawings of the same shoes see Figs. 56, 49, 42, 54.

three further shoes which differ considerably from any of those discussed so far and which can more properly be regarded as prototypes of the most important styles of the late 14th century. The soles are quite sharply pointed at the toe, and the uppers are of two-part construction. One is laced at the front, the second has a latchet fastening, and the third has a buckle. The front-laced shoe is illustrated and described in detail below (Fig. 52 and p. 34).

The late 14th century (Fig. 41)

It is to this period that the largest and by far the best preserved group of footwear ever to have been recovered from a London site belongs. There are 417 registered shoes of this date from 'Baynards Castle', and it is clear that most were discarded when complete and relatively undamaged. Such is the quality of the preservation that many details of wear and texture, which are lost on leatherwork from other deposits, can still be seen and evaluated. The only other group of

precisely the same period comes from the neighbouring site of Trig Lane, but although quite large (70 registered shoes), it is so poorly preserved that only the most general comparisons can be made with the 'Baynards Castle' finds.

As can be seen from Table 6, 'Baynards Castle' is unique among London assemblages in that below-the-ankle shoes are by far the most common form of footwear, accounting for as much as 81 per cent of the combined shoes, ankle-shoes and boots total; ankle-shoes amount to just 17 per cent, and boots to a mere 2 per cent. The shoes were mostly fastened across the instep, either with a buckle or with a latchet – a bifurcated leather strap passed through a pair of holes – whereas the ankle-shoes and boots were normally laced, either at the front or at the side. The Trig Lane assemblage, on the other hand, contains a much higher proportion of boots and ankle-shoes (Table 7), and even among the fragments too small for attribution to a particular type of footwear there are no certain examples of buckles or of the side-latchet fastening. Instead, front-laced and side-laced fragments are the main constituents. Some of the former are from children's shoes (see below and Figs. 53–4) but others are probably from adult ankle-shoes of a type com-

Table 6. Shoes (all sizes) from 'Baynards Castle', late 14th century.

	Buckle	Front-laced	Side-laced	Front-latchet	Side-latchet	Buckle or latchet	Toggle	Not known	Total
Shoe	51	11	2	44	30	25	2	37	202
Ankle-shoe	4	17	12	1	—	1	1	8	44
Boot	—	—	4	—	—	—	—	2	6
Not known	18	10	1	14	2	18	—	102	165
Total	73	38	19	57	32	44	3	149	417

Table 7. Shoes (all sizes) from Trig Lane, late 14th century.

	Buckle	Front-laced	Side-laced	Front-latchet	Side-latchet	Buckle or latchet	Toggle	Not known	Total
Shoe	—	—	—	1	—	—	—	4	5
Ankle-shoe	—	1	8	—	—	—	—	—	9
Boot	—	1	6	—	—	—	—	—	7
Not known	—	19	5	10	—	4	—	11	49
Total	—	21	19	11	—	4	—	15	70

paratively rare at 'Baynards Castle' (*cf.* Figs. 55 & 58); and the high proportion of the latter – almost invariably from ankle-shoes or boots – could be regarded as part of a broader trend whereby this type of footwear steadily increased in popularity from the mid 14th to the early 15th centuries (*cf.* Tables 5 and 11).

If, therefore, the Trig Lane group seems to fit the pattern established from other London sites, 'Baynards Castle' is clearly at variance with it. Seasonal factors might be held partially responsible – perhaps shoes were worn more often in summer and boots or ankle-shoes in winter – but the distinctive nature of the assemblage is emphasised still further by the fact that very few of the soles have been repaired: fewer than 9 per cent of the total, compared with a range of 35–50 per cent in other London groups (*cf.* p. 89–90 and Table 15). This could imply that the shoes came from households that were rather wealthier than average, or even possibly, in a few cases, from the Royal Wardrobe, which in the 14th century lay just to the north of the 'Baynards Castle' site. Consistent with this is the observation that many shoes are quite remarkably pointed, a feature that doubtless could have been afforded only by the more fashion-conscious elements in society.

As shown above (p. 26), a rather broad, rounded toe style was favoured in the mid 14th century, but in the last quarter of the century almost every type of shoe was at least slightly pointed. This can be seen from Table 8, which is an expression of the ratio between the length of the shoe beyond the end of the foot and the length of the foot itself, as estimated from impressions left by the toes or ball of the foot; the ratio is tabulated, first, in conjunction with the fastening types (8a) and, secondly, in comparison with the actual foot lengths converted to their modern shoe size equivalents (8b). From this it can be seen that side-laced boots and front-laced shoes or ankle-shoes seem to have had the shortest points – no more than would be consistent with their suggested workaday function – and that low-cut, buckled or latchet-fastened shoes seem to have had the longest (Table 8a). At 'Baynards Castle', these 'poulaines', which were notorious in their day and are well documented in contemporary literature and illustrations (see below, pp. 115–7), sometimes reached a length of over 100 mm and were normally stuffed with moss or hair so as to retain their shape. Even some of the tiniest children's shoes had quite pronounced points (*cf.* Figs. 53–4), although, as might be expected, the

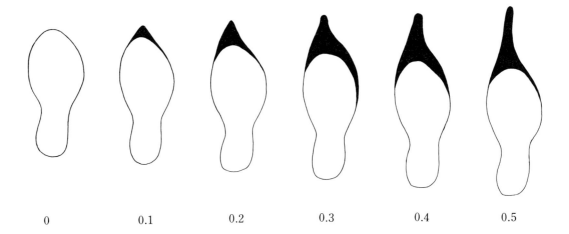

0	0.1	0.2	0.3	0.4	0.5

(a)

	0	0.1	0.2	0.3	0.4	0.5	Total
child's 1	—	4	1	—	—	—	5
2	—	—	1	—	—	—	1
3	1	—	—	—	—	—	1
4	3	1	—	—	—	—	4
5	1	—	1	—	—	—	2
6	2	2	2	—	—	—	6
7	—	—	2	—	—	—	2
8	—	—	1	—	—	—	1
9	—	—	—	—	—	—	—
10	2	3	2	—	—	—	7
11	1	1	3	—	—	—	5
12	—	1	3	1	—	—	5
13	1	3	5	—	—	—	9
adult 1	—	1	18	2	—	1	22
2	1	6	14	2	—	2	25
3	—	6	14	2	2	1	25
4	4	6	14	2	1	2	29
5	3	7	8	8	3	—	29
6	5	4	2	2	1	1	15
7	2	3	1	1	1	—	8
8	6	2	1	—	—	—	9
Total	32	50	93	20	8	7	210

(b)

	0	0.1	0.2	0.3	0.4	0.5	Total
Buckle	6	7	23	3	1	1	41
Front-laced	4	10	11	—	—	—	25
Side-laced	1	3	7	—	—	—	11
Front-latchet	5	13	24	1	—	—	43
Side-latchet	3	4	2	4	3	2	18
Buckle or latchet	1	3	11	1	2	1	19
Toggle	1	1	—	—	—	—	2
Not known	11	9	15	11	2	3	51
Total	32	50	93	20	8	7	210

Table 8: shoes from 'Baynards Castle', late 14th century. The popularity of the 'poulaine' – albeit of modest proportions – can be judged from this table, which is an expression of the ratio between the length of the shoe beyond the position of the toes (estimated by impressions on the sole) and the length of the wearer's foot. This ratio, calculated as a fraction, can be compared with (a) the shoe sizes according to the modern English Shoe Size Scales (see below, pp. 102–5) and (b) the style of shoe.

longest are associated exclusively with the adult sizes (Table 8b). Occasionally the 'poulaine' has been deliberately cut off (*cf.* Fig. 50) – perhaps because the wearer no longer found it comfortable and wished to convert an old shoe, that had once been his 'best', into something more suitable for everyday use. In the Trig Lane group, however, shoes and boots of all kinds are much less pointed, and there are no 'poulaines' which exceed a length of *c*.40 mm.

It was perhaps the low sides and the excessive length of some 'poulaines' which caused the tradi-

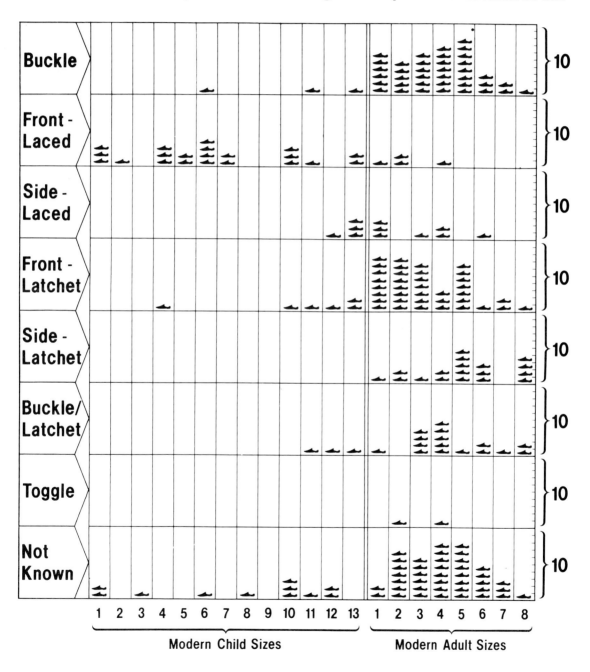

tional 'wrap-around' method to be abandoned for the making of shoes and it to be replaced by a very standardised two-part system in which the vamp and quarters were separate units joined by symmetrical seams on either side. Among the shoes from 'Baynards Castle' there is only one made in one piece, and that is for a very small child (Fig. 53). Ankle-shoes and boots, however, continued to be made in the traditional way. A further innovation was the addition of a tongue, similar to that on a modern shoe, to front-laced shoes and ankle-shoes which had a deep opening at the vamp throat. This was usually sewn along just one edge (*cf.* Fig. 98), and would not only have made the upper more waterproof but would have prevented the lace from chafing on the instep. As at all periods, decoration is rare. There is just one example of openwork decoration – the quarters of a low-cut shoe (see below, pp. 80–1 and Fig. 115c) – but from 'Baynards Castle' there are several magnificently-engraved designs composed either of geometric or of foliate motifs (Figs. 50–51; below, pp. 83–7). It was probably so as to protect shoes like these that wooden overshoes – 'pattens' – first came into more general use (see below, pp. 91–6).

Nearly all shoes had buckle or latchet fastenings (Tables 6–7) and were very similar in styling (Figs. 42–47; 49–51). They were invariably cut low at the sides beneath the arch of the foot, and, except for one of the latchet types (the 'side-latchet'), the quarters were normally shaped in an elegant curve below the ankle on the outer side but left horizontal on the inner. For convenience, the strap or latchet was normally sewn to the inner side, and the buckle or latchet-holes set on the outer, where they would be more accessible. In constructional details also they were virtually identical: they had no topband or heel-reinforcement, but a cord was stitched to the inside of the quarters around the ankle and to the inside of the vamp as far as the toes in order to protect the leather from stretching and chafing at the weakest points (*cf.* Figs. 102–104). As Table 9 shows, these styles were worn almost exclusively by older children and adults. And to judge from the complete examples, where the sole survives intact for measurement, it seems that buckled shoes were proportionally more common than front-

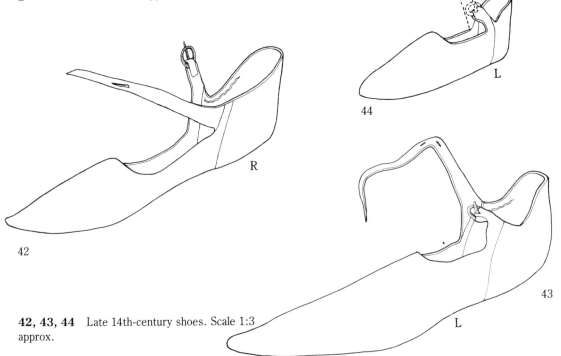

42, 43, 44 Late 14th-century shoes. Scale 1:3 approx.

latchet shoes in the larger adult sizes. From this it might be inferred that they were worn more often by men, whereas the front-latchet type, which has a more even spread of adult sizes, was worn equally by both sexes. But side-latchet shoes are found in the largest sizes of all, leaving little doubt that this was principally a man's shoe; it may equally be significant that the longest 'poulaines' (Table 8a) and the finest examples of decoration (Figs. 50–51) are also associated with shoes of this type.

The adult buckled shoes which are illustrated are typical of the whole collection (Figs. 42–3). Both have circular buckles of tinned iron which are held in place by folding over the leather strap on the outer side and stitching it down; the strap which passes over the instep is a separate insert. One shoe (Fig. 42) has only a modest 'poulaine' and, although originally high over the instep like the other, has been cut down – perhaps by a particularly fashion-conscious owner – so that it barely covers the toes (*cf.* Figs. 49–51). One of the front-latchet shoes is similar to these in that the vamp continues high over the instep and there is only a short 'poulaine' (Fig. 45). The bifurcated latchet strap is a separate insert, and the strap with the corresponding pair of holes is made in one piece with the vamp; it is of single thickness but with a reinforcement cord just inside the edge. The other adult front-latchet shoe (Fig. 46) is cut lower over the toes and has a slightly longer, outward-curving 'poulaine'. Unusually, there is a small insert to join the vamp and quarters on the inner side and, as on several other examples of this type, the short perforated strap is a separate insert folded double and sewn together at the edges. The ends of the latchet strap remain knotted together, but on some other surviving examples each strand was knotted individually after passing through the hole, in the manner of a toggle.

The illustrated side-latchet shoes emphasise the high fashion associated with this style (Figs. 49–51). All are cut very low across the toes and at the sides, but the quarters are not shaped; unlike the front-latchet shoes, they were generally fastened on the inner, not the outer, side of the foot. The latchet strap itself was invariably made separately, and because of the length of the shoe the sole was normally made in two parts. The plain shoe (Fig. 49) has one of the longest 'poulaines' in

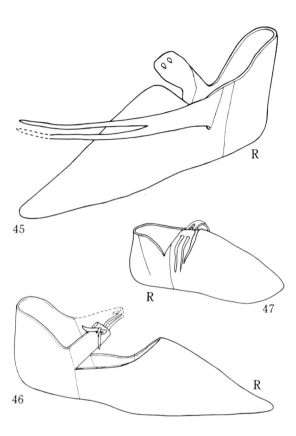

45, 46, 47   Late 14th-century shoes. Scale 1:3 approx.

the entire 'Baynards Castle' group, extending to over 120 mm, and the seam on the outer side is reinforced with a large rectangular patch, probably stitched on as a repair; this seam would have been exposed to considerable stress, since it lies at the point of greatest flexibility and is very short in comparison with the overall size of the shoe. The decorated shoes are very similar in style, although one (Fig. 50) is slightly shaped at the quarters and is cut very low over the toes; a rough slit has been made, perhaps to give more room for the toes, and the end of the 'poulaine' has been cut off. Both shoes are similarly decorated with scored lines and areas where the surface has been scraped away to provide a contrasting 'suede' finish, but the effects are very different. One (Fig. 50) is very light in appearance, with an overall lattice-work enclosing 'suede' lozenges, whereas the

48 Late 14th-century shoes decorated with engraved and scraped motifs. The 'poulaine' of one shoe seems to have been cut off deliberately. For line drawings of the same shoes see Figs. 121a, 50 & 51.

other (Fig. 51) is divided by 'suede' bands into a series of dark rectangular panels relieved only by very fine cross-hatching.

Adult shoes were occasionally fastened by lacing at the front, providing a firmer fit over the instep and sides of the foot. This was not done as on a modern shoe but by an extension of the latchet principle, for it is clear that the intention was for the lace to remain fixed on one side of the vamp opening and to be threaded through holes in the other, where it could be tied. In some instances a bifurcated latchet-type tag seems to have been provided (*cf.* below and Fig. 55) but in others – as with the illustrated example (Fig. 52) – the lace was a single narrow strip of leather squeezed through the holes on one side at exactly its mid point. On the same side as the lace was fixed, a tongue was sewn edge-to-edge along the slit; this then passed below the opposite pair of holes to give protection to the instep as that side was manipulated and the lace tightened during

fastening. The sole of the shoe is heavily worn, and a very large repair piece was added, which enveloped the whole of the underside to the extent that it was sewn to the lower parts of the upper. This accounts for the rather unusual appearance of a shoe which in many other respects resembles the standard buckled and latchet types: in its two-part construction, in the absence of a heel-stiffener or topband, and in the shaping of the quarters – in this case below both ankles – together with the use of a reinforcement cord.

To judge by the evidence from 'Baynards Castle', small children's shoes were very similar to those worn by adolescents and adults, although the proportion of ankle-shoes seems to have been slightly higher than average and there are no exaggerated 'poulaines' (*cf.* Table 8b). Of the 19 complete soles where the actual foot length can be estimated at less than 170 mm (notionally equivalent to the modern child's size 9 or smaller), 9 belong to below-the-ankle shoes, 6 to ankle-shoes and 7 to indeterminate types. But as is evident from Table 9, small children's shoes of all types differed to the extent that almost invariably they were fastened by lacing at the front. There is a

49, 50, 51 Late 14th-century shoes. Scale 1:3 approx.

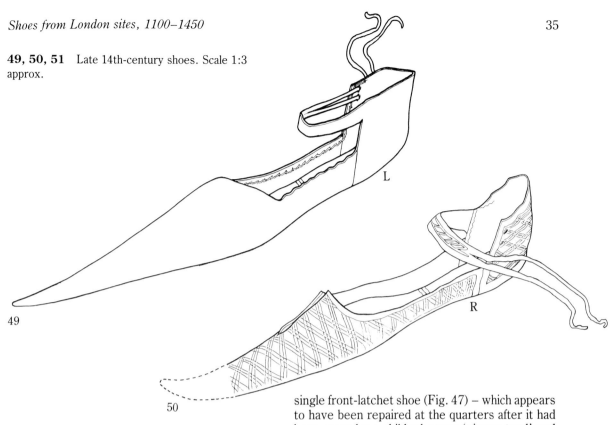

49

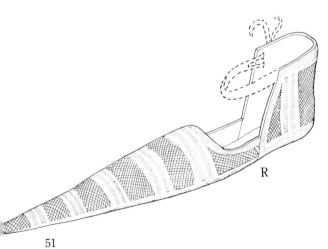

50

51

single front-latchet shoe (Fig. 47) – which appears to have been repaired at the quarters after it had been worn by a child who was 'pigeon-toed' and whose foot pushed it abnormally outwards (see further, below, pp. 107–8) – and a single shoe fastened with a buckle (Fig. 44). The buckle, now mostly lost, is of lead alloy rather than iron, but in styling and construction the shoe is an exact miniature of the adult versions. The front-laced shoes also have much in common with the front-laced shoes discussed above (*cf.* Figs. 52–4), although none of the surviving examples seem to have had tongues. One of those illustrated (Fig. 53) is unique in the present collection in that it is of one-piece construction. The lace, which is knotted at each end, passes from above through the holes on the side where it is fastened, not from below as

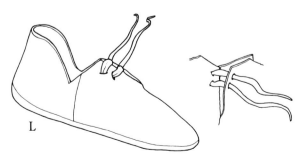

52 Mid 14th-century shoe. Scale 1:3 approx.

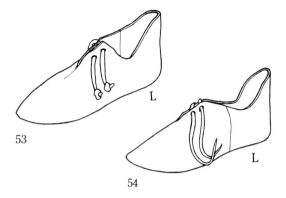

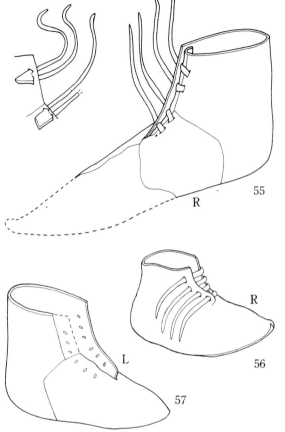

53, 54 Late 14th-century shoes. Scale 1:3 approx.

seems to have been more common. Most shoes of this type were only slightly pointed at the toe, but the second illustrated example (Fig. 54) has a tiny 'poulaine' stuffed with hair – perhaps human hair. In this instance the lace is of the bifurcated 'latchet' type.

It remains to discuss the ankle-shoes and low boots which are a smaller and much less distinctive part, at least of the 'Baynards Castle' assemblage. Buckled ankle-shoes were found in very small numbers (Table 6) and are described in detail below (p. 41), since they anticipate a fashion of the early 15th century. Of the other two main methods of fastening, side-lacing appears to have been marginally less common (Tables 6–7), and the examples of this date are so similar in construction and styling to those of both earlier and later times – except insofar as they may have modest 'poulaines' – that no further description is necessary. It was during this period, however, that front-lacing seems first to have developed as an important method for fastening ankle-shoes; and as with front-laced shoes, a modification of the latchet principle was adopted.

The illustrated ankle-shoe (Fig. 55) and the low boot (Fig. 58) share a similar one-piece 'wrap-around' construction, with an angled main seam on the inner side. There was a heel-stiffener but no topband, and large reinforcement-pieces were secured on the inside to protect the area around the lace-holes. On the boot this can be seen only from impressions and stitch-marks, but on the ankle-shoe, which is much better preserved, the reinforcements partially survive in place (*cf.* Fig.

55, 56, 57 Late 14th-century ankle-shoes. Scale 1:3 approx.

100); one is a simple strip, probably applied after the shoe had been assembled, but the other is much more substantial and is an integral part of the construction, being attached by the main seam. The lace-holes on either side of the ankle-shoe are arranged in two pairs, corresponding to a pair of bifurcated latchet-type tags which remain intact on the inner side; the tongue, which rose to the full height of the shoe, was sewn edge-to-edge along this side also (Fig. 55). The fastening arrangements on the boot are not entirely clear, since on the surviving side there are seven lace-holes, evenly spaced. The small child's ankle-shoe (Fig. 56) and the child's boot (Fig. 57) are almost identical in style to their adult counterparts, although there seem to have been no heel-stiffeners, lace-hole reinforcements or tongues.

58 Late 14th-century boot. Scale 1:3 approx.

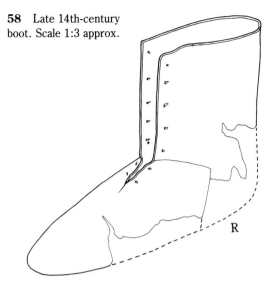

The early 15th century (Fig. 59)

The latest shoes from the London waterfront belong to the first half of the 15th century and were found in three deposits. The condition of the leather and of the metal fittings is generally quite good, but there are far fewer complete shoes than in the preceding 'Baynards Castle' group and it seems that many were already in pieces (though not, apparently, deliberately cut up) when thrown away. One of the groups, from Swan Lane, is slightly earlier than the others and is best considered separately. It is also by far the smallest (15 registered shoes). The other two groups are very large indeed and roughly contemporary: one, also from Swan Lane, contains 109 registered shoes, the other, from Trig Lane, 359 registered shoes.

There is little perceptible difference in composition between the earlier of the Swan Lane groups and the large late 14th-century groups which preceded it (see above, pp. 28–36). The

59 Early 15th-century boot and ankle-shoes. One (bottom left) was certainly fastened with a buckle (now missing) and another (top centre) may have been. The third (bottom right) was laced at the side, and stitching shows that originally it had a repair sole. For line drawings of the same or similar shoes see Figs. 67, 63 & 69.

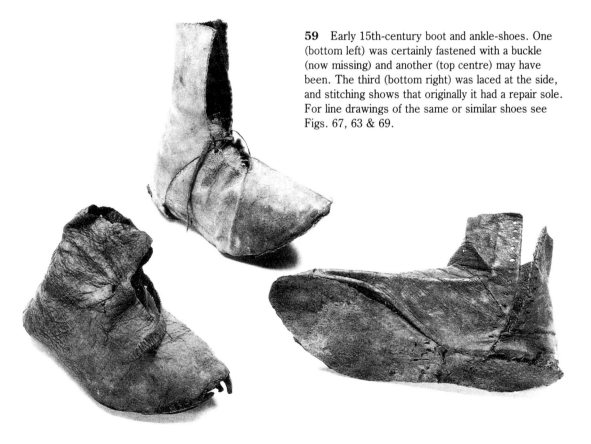

toes are almost invariably pointed, sometimes with quite exaggerated 'poulaines'; low-cut shoes outnumber ankle-shoes and boots; and latchets and buckles are the only fastening types definitely identified. The most distinctive item, apparently unparalleled either in earlier or in later deposits, is a large ankle-shoe with a baggy, moss-stuffed 'poulaine' (Fig. 60). It has no topband or heel-stiffener and was made symmetrically in two parts: the quarters, which were joined by a vertical seam at the heel, were sewn to the vamp with a single seam running continuously across the instep from one side to the other. This form of construction, which leaves no natural opening at the side or vamp throat, removes the need for fastening, and so it is almost certain that the shoe was worn as a slip-on. The metal fittings, one of iron, the other of lead alloy, which are rivetted through the leather, are badly corroded but seem to have been ornamental studs rather than buckles.

During the twenty or thirty years that elapsed between the deposition of this group and the deposition of the later Swan Lane and Trig Lane groups important changes in style and construction seem to have taken place. Broad, rounded toes once more returned to fashion for shoes of every kind – although moss stuffing was some-times still used to give a more even profile and to keep the toe of the shoe in shape – and ankle-shoes or boots again came to outnumber by far the low-cut shoes. This is demonstrated by Tables 10 and 11, where it can be seen that at both Trig Lane and Swan Lane buckled or latchet-fastened shoes of the same general type as found in the late 14th century, but without 'poulaines', are a tiny com-

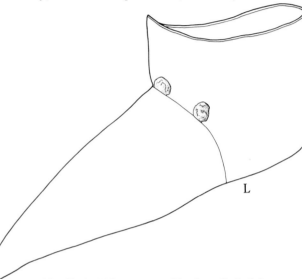

60 Early 15th-century ankle-shoe. Scale 1:3 approx.

Table 10. Shoes (all sizes) from Swan Lane, early/mid 15th century.

	Buckle	Front-laced	Side-laced	Front-latchet	Side-latchet	Buckle or latchet	Not known	Total
Shoe	2	—	—	—	1	—	—	3
Ankle-shoe	8	1	—	—	—	—	1	10
Boot	5	—	16	—	—	—	—	21
Not known	10	2	25	—	—	1	37	75
Total	25	3	41	—	1	1	38	109

Table 11. Shoes (all sizes) from Trig Lane, early/mid 15th century.

	Buckle	Front-laced	Side-laced	Front-latchet	Side-latchet	Buckle or latchet	Not known	Total
Shoe	2	—	—	—	2	4	3	11
Ankle-shoe	38	5	36	—	—	—	15	94
Boot	4	—	73	—	—	—	5	82
Not known	32	5	80	—	—	3	52	172
Total	76	10	189	—	2	7	75	359

ponent of the assemblages. These may have been replaced in part by a new type of all-leather patten which, it is suggested (*cf.* below, p. 101 and Figs. 139–40), were not worn as overshoes but simply over the hose. Among the shoes themselves two very different types are dominant which, when allowance is made for the large number of uncertain fragments, were probably present at both sites in similar proportions. One, the side-laced ankle-shoe or boot (boots reaching about a third of the height to the knee seem to have been the more common fashion), was a style which had a long ancestry, albeit in a less standardised form and with slight differences in construction. The other, the front-opening buckled ankle-shoe or low boot, was an entirely new style, although it perhaps should be regarded as a replacement for the front-laced ankle-shoe of the late 14th century with which it shared many features of design and construction, both overall and in detail.

But it was the technical developments of the early 15th century which are of the greatest significance. In the construction of some ankle-shoe uppers the two-part method was taken a stage

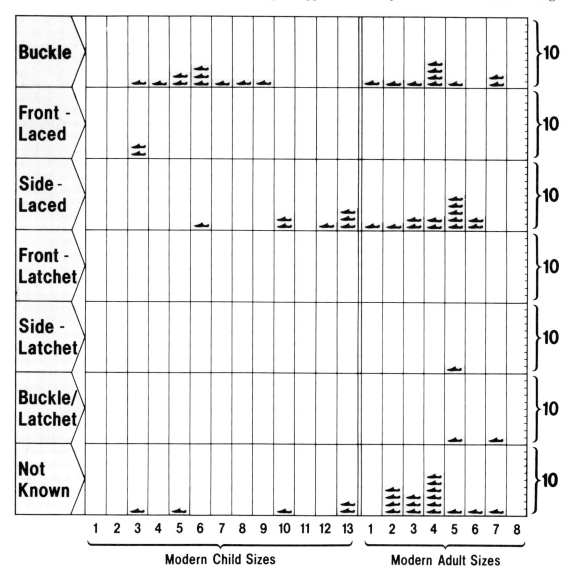

further so that the quarters were made in two symmetrical pieces – now properly 'quarters' in the modern sense – and joined with a vertical seam at the heel (Figs. 67 and 107). This added considerably to the importance of the heel-stiffener, making it an integral constructional element, and anticipates the sophisticated construction of 17th-century and later shoes. It is noticeable that when compared with 13th- and 14th-century examples far fewer early 15th-century uppers have been cut up for subsequent reuse (*c.*10 per cent, compared with 20–45 per cent in earlier groups; *cf.*, below, Table 16), and this may indicate that shoes were now made throughout of new, rather than recycled, leather.

At the same time there seem to have been two major advances in sole manufacture, although the paucity of examples in the present groups suggests that the changes were taking place at just the period when the groups themselves were being deposited. One advance, exemplified by only 5 of the 359 registered shoes from Trig Lane and none from Swan Lane, was the addition of a separate insole to the normal turn-shoe sole. The insole lay grain-side upwards and must have added considerably to the comfort of the shoe. The other advance was the introduction of the turn-welt method of construction (for fuller discussion, see below, p. 47 & Fig. 74). This involved the widening of the normal turn-shoe rand so that it oversailed the edge of the shoe and could be sewn to a separate undersole, thereby improving greatly the durability of the whole shoe and its resistance to water. There are no examples of turn-welt shoes among the individually registered finds, although several scraps of turn-welt 'rand', easily recognised by the double row of stitch-holes, were located in the bulk material. When found separately, the lower soles may be difficult to distinguish from well-made 'clumps' if they are tunnel-stitched, and from the bottom components of multi-layer pattens (see below, Figs. 139–40) if through-stitched.

Decoration is sparse on London shoes of this period, although there is one vamp with magnificent 'tracery' ornament reminiscent of the architecture and metalwork of the time (Fig. 116c). Too little of the upper survives for certain reconstruction, but it seems likely that it was a low-cut shoe with buckle or latchet fastening. Distinctive touches were sometimes added to a shoe by

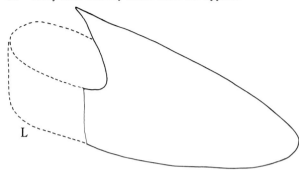

61 Early 15th-century shoe. Scale 1:3 approx.

simple variations in cutting and stitching. Two vamps, for example – again probably from below-the-ankle shoes – are shaped very low at the wings but have a long pointed 'tongue' which extends upwards over the instep (Fig. 61). Another vamp has two rows of longitudinal tunnel-stitching on the inside, which had the effect of creasing the vamp to create a slightly stepped, rather than rounded, profile (Fig. 62). Regrettably little of this shoe survives, but there are remains of a strap passing through a perforation at the vamp throat; this suggests that it had a toggle fastening, although if so it would be the only example from a London context post-dating *c.*1400.

62 Early 15th-century shoe. As can be seen from the illustration of the inside (flesh side) of the vamp, the longitudinal creases were formed by two rows of tunnel-stitching. Scale 1:3 approx (inset 1:4).

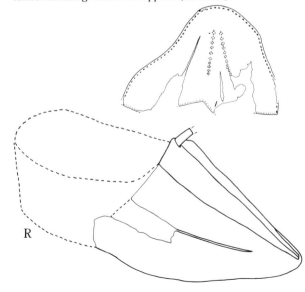

Front-laced ankle-shoes and boots seem to have been worn but rarely in the first half of the 15th century (Tables 10–11), and then only by very small children (*cf.* Table 12). They were identical in style and construction to the late 14th-century examples discussed above (p. 36 and Fig. 56). Much more popular, and differing significantly only in respect of the fastening method, was the buckled ankle-shoe (Tables 10–11). As Table 12 shows – although it must be remembered that the total of measurable examples is small and that as many as three of the adult fragments may be from shoes rather than ankle-shoes – the type has an unusual size distribution, being concentrated in the infant and adult ranges. This suggests that it may have been worn mainly by men and very young children, perhaps because of its essentially practical and sturdy design.

Buckled ankle-shoes were invariably made by the 'wrap-around' method, normally with the main seam on the inner side. Sometimes a single piece of leather was sufficient (Fig. 63), but more often a small insert was required to raise the inner side to its full height (Figs. 64–5). There was generally

a heel-stiffener but no topband. The tongues rarely survive, but those that do (*cf.* Fig. 64) seem to have been stitched to one side only of the vamp opening; on the other side was probably a reinforcement cord. The buckle, which was fixed to a leather thong, and its corresponding strap passed through slots on either side of the vamp opening and were secured inside (see further, p. 75). In the late 14th century buckles had nearly all been of tinned iron, but now they were almost always of lead and more ornamental. Some were decorated with beading at the edge, and 'spectacle' buckles made their first appearance (see below, pp. 75–6 and Fig. 110). Whereas the children's ankle-shoes seldom had more than a single buckle, the adult version was often provided with a pair (Fig. 66). An unusual feature of the illustrated example is that it did not have a normal tongue, but instead, to judge by the presence of a butt seam along both edges of the vamp opening (*cf.* Fig. 106), there was an insert sewn flush to make the shoe entirely enclosed and waterproof; this insert, now missing, was presumably made of soft flexible leather so that when the wearer had put the shoe on, he could gather it tightly over the instep with the buckles.

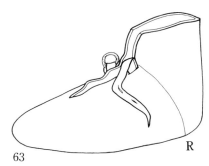

63

R

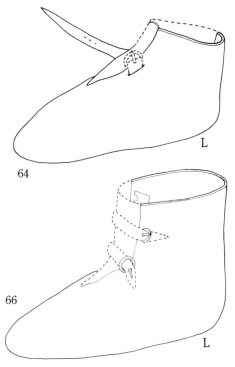

64

L

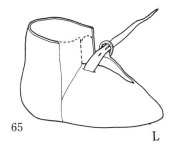

65

L

66

L

63, 64, 65, 66 Early 15th-century ankle-shoes. Scale 1:3 approx.

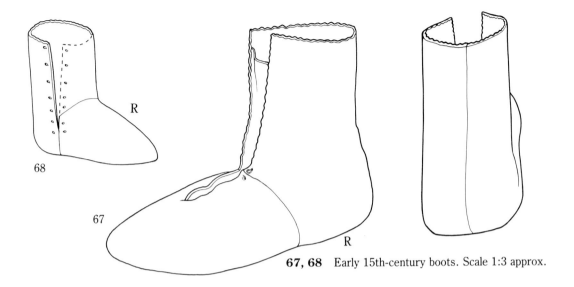

67, 68   Early 15th-century boots. Scale 1:3 approx.

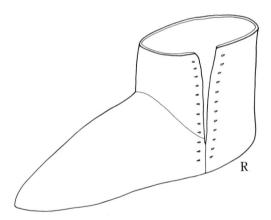

69   Early 15th-century ankle-shoe. Scale 1:3 approx.

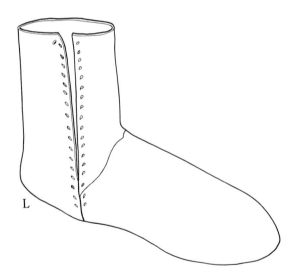

70   Early 15th-century boot. Scale 1:3 approx.

A further type of buckled footwear, this time a low boot, has so far been found only in the adult sizes. None of the surviving examples has a complete sole, but the uppers all seem to have been made from three basic components – a vamp and two quarters – joined at the heel and with symmetrical curving seams on either side (Fig. 67). There was a heel-stiffener and a topband, which evidently continued down each edge of the front opening as far as the instep and thereafter only along the edge on the outer side (*cf.* Fig. 107); affixed to the inner side, a short distance inside the edge, was a tongue which reached to within *c.*40 mm of the top of the boot. An unusual feature for a boot of this size is the provision of only one pair of small round perforations for fastening straps, at the point where the vamp is angled sharply from the horizontal to the vertical planes. On the illustrated example they are empty, but on a second, almost identical fragment they carry a small buckle and strap which would have had the effect of fastening the boot tightly at the ankle, while leaving it loose at the top.

By far the most common form of footwear in the early 15th century was the side-laced ankle-shoe or boot (Tables 10–11), a style seen regularly on monumental brasses and illustrations of the time (see below, p. 118 & Fig. 159). To judge by the examples in the present collection, they were worn only seldom by very young children but otherwise were produced throughout the whole range of older children's, women's and men's sizes (Table 12). The heights vary considerably,

from quite low ankle-shoes (Fig. 69) to boots rising to *c.*220 mm – mid-calf height; but more moderate proportions, similar to those of the illustrated boot (Fig. 70), seem to have been the most common. The lace-holes are normally very closely spaced, including more than 40 pairs on the tallest boots, but since none of the laces remain in place it is not known exactly how they were fastened.

The smallest ankle-shoes were often made, as in the early 14th century, by the 'wrap-around' method with a single insert at the instep (Fig. 68), but most of the remainder share a mass-produced, tripartite construction. The three parts – vamp, one-piece quarters and insert at the front – were almost symmetrical in plan (see Fig. 108) and were joined by symmetrically-placed seams on either side and at the instep. A heel-stiffener was sometimes added, but a topband only rarely (*cf.* Fig. 68). There was no tongue to cover the side opening, but reinforcement-pieces were invariably sewn on the inside to strengthen the lace-holes. The side opening itself must always have been a point of severe weakness because it reached so far down that the main seam connecting the vamp and quarters was never more than 5 or 6 stitches long. This may account for the fact that hardly any side-laced boots or ankle-shoes have survived complete and may also have contributed to the apparent demise of the type in the later 15th and 16th centuries. These developments, however, which are poorly represented by finds from London, exceed the scope of the present survey.

Shoemaking and cobbling

In most villages of the realm there is some dresser or worker of leather, and for the supplies of such as have not, there are in most market towns three, four or five, and in many great towns or cities 10 or 20, and in London and its suburbs nearly 200.

(BL Lansdowne Ms. 74 No. 154, quoted in Thomas 1983, 2)

The Leather

There were several long processes which had to be gone through before a shoemaker could begin his work. The tanner would buy hides from the butcher with hooves and horns still attached. The skins were then washed, trimmed, had the hair removed and, finally, were tanned (for full accounts of the process, see Thomas 1983; Salzman 1923). Leather identification (by Glynis Edwards of the Ancient Monuments Laboratory), which has been done on over sixty shoes spanning the full date range of the collection (Table 13), as well as less precise visual and tactile examination, indicates that there was a change in the types of hides used for the uppers, probably at some time in the 13th century. Instead of cattle hide, the earlier shoes are biased towards sheep/goat (cordwain) – although it should be noted that Edwards states in her report (1986) that 'some of those described as sheep/goat may have been

deer, but we are not yet certain of the diagnostic pattern of the latter' (*cf*. Reed 1972, 285 for similarities between sheep/goat and deer). Calf

71 Shoemakers and cobblers at work. *a*: Cutting out an upper. The half-moon-shaped knife was normally used for this purpose. *b*: Use of the awl to make holes, apparently in preparation for stitching the lasting-margin. Beside the shoemaker's stool is a pair of lasts. His products clearly included side-laced boots (cf. Figs. 68–70). *c*: Sewing. The craftsman, in this case a cobbler, appears to be working on the lasting-margin and, having just completed a stitch, is pulling the two threads firmly apart (cf. Fig. 73). *d*: Trimming. The shoemaker uses a small, angled-back knife to finish a virtually-completed shoe; it is possible that he is paring away the rough edges of the lasting-margin. A pair of lasts lies in a rack on the wall. (From the Mendel Housebook (Nuremberg), 15th century).

Table 13.   The types of leather used in medieval shoes. Details of individual shoes are given in the List of Figures and Concordance (pp. 126–30).

	Uppers (vamps and/or quarters)			Heel-stiffeners			Total
	sheep/goat	calf	not known	sheep/goat	calf	not known	
Mid 12th c.	4	1	—	—	—	—	5
Late 12th c.	—	3	—	1	—	—	4
Early/mid 13th c.	8	4	—	—	—	—	12
Late 13th/early 14th c.	—	3	2	1	—	—	6
Mid 14th c.	1	4	—	1	1	—	7
Late 14th c.	2	19	1	—	2	—	24
Early/mid 15th c.	2	9	—	—	2	—	13
Not stratified	—	3	—	—	—	—	3
Total	17	46	3	3	5	—	74

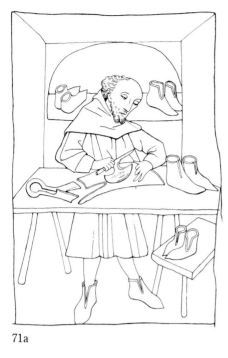

71a

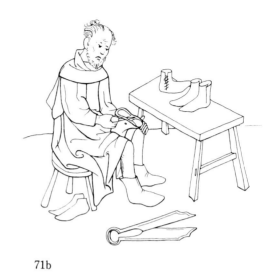

71b

71c

71d

easily predominates amongst the sampled uppers from the mid 13th century onwards, though occasional examples of sheep/goat were found in all groups. Toggle and latchet thongs with an identifiable grain pattern were found to be calf, contrasting with Goubitz's suggestion that these were more likely to be sheep/goat because of the strength and flexibility of that leather (O. Goubitz, pers. comm.) Heel-stiffeners were both calf and sheep/goat, the latter not occurring after the mid 14th century. At least two shoes (Fig. 13, late 12th-century; Fig. 39, mid 14th-century) may have had calfskin uppers and sheep or goatskin heel-stiffeners – an intriguing commentary on a clause in some ordinances of the London Cordwainers' Company (dated 1303; Mander 1931, 33–4) that expressly forbade shoemakers to mix materials on the same shoe.

One theory that has been advanced for the change in the types of hides used is that the method of tannage had been changed; but Roy Thompson, himself a tanner, believes that tanning remained largely unchanged from the Saxon period to the 16th or 17th centuries, with tanners mainly using oak (though slipping in whatever else they thought they could get away with). The increased use of calf may, on the one hand, have

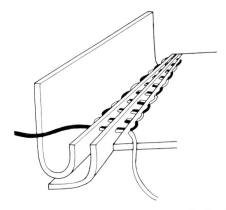

73 Turn-shoe construction with rand. The lasting-margin has been sewn with edge/flesh stitches for the sole and grain/flesh for the upper and rand.

been due to stricter control by the leathermakers' guilds, but, on the other, may have been the result of a decrease in the amount of imported goatskin, or cordwain, from Spain following the expulsion of the Moors. English tanners and shoemakers responded by attempting to duplicate the effect of the imported cordwain with calf hide which they dyed a reddish colour (June Swann, pers. comm). A further possible explanation may lie in the introduction in the late 14th century of organised drives of cattle to the London markets; this will have ensured a constant supply of cattle hides in the City, whereas previously the London shoemakers would have had to use whatever they could get (Philip Armitage, pers. comm.). The 15th-century material in the present collection shows a decrease both in the number of uppers that have been repaired (Table 15) and in the number that have been deliberately cut up for reuse (Table 16), facts that might be attributable to better-quality and more organised supplies of leather being available to shoemakers and cobblers.

Shoemaking

The tanned hides of goat, deer or calf which had been purchased by the shoemaker would be laid flat and the shoes planned to ensure the maximum number with the minimum wastage. There is evidence from Sweden that cutting patterns were used to guide the knife through the thickness of the leather (June Swann, pers. comm), although it is possible that a very skilled craftsman could perform the task freehand. Certainly the quantity

72 Turn-shoe construction without rand. From the mid 12th century onwards the sole was invariably attached with edge/flesh stitches; the upper occasionally had edge/flesh stitches likewise (cf. Fig. 76), but grain/flesh stitches (as shown here) were more common. (NB. In this and Figs. 73–4 the seam is drawn 'opened up', *not* as if it were in the process of being sewn; that, of course, would have been done when the shoe was turned inside out.)

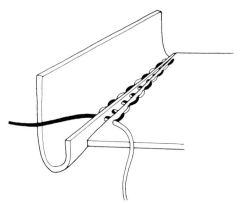

of long narrow trimming pieces that have been found on London sites seems to indicate that, whatever the method, the results were not always precise; and besides, some of the small inserts stitched into uppers are more likely the result of miscalculation than of design.

Once cut to shape, the shoe was moulded on a last, a wooden form that served as a model of the foot (*cf.* Fig. 71b; for two examples from York, see MacGregor 1982, 144–5 and Fig. 74). The last probably was not always an exact model of the foot but may often have been adapted to suit the demands of current fashion and preference (*cf.* Salaman 1986, 144–5). After moulding and stitching, which was done with it inside-out, the shoe was then turned right-side out: hence the name 'turn-shoe'. Although present-day shoemakers now specialise in particular aspects of the craft, it is probable that in the medieval period the entire process was carried out by a single craftsman (*ibid.*, 20). Indeed ordinances passed in 1272 forbidding cordwainers to tan leather and tanners to make shoes imply that some members of the craft followed the whole process through from tanning the hides to making and selling the shoes (Mander 1931, 28–30). Despite a general adherence to certain styles, there are likely to have been differences in techniques and practices between one shoemaker and another, and this is perhaps shown by the variations to be observed amongst styles which are superficially the same (compare, for example, Figs. 89 and 90).

Throughout the period represented by the present collection, the method of making a turn-shoe remained relatively consistent, with the main variations occurring in the cutting and planning. Leaving aside the earliest shoe (Fig. 82), which follows the 11th-century tradition in having the lasting-margin inset from the sole edge (see further, Pritchard forthcoming), it seems that most 12th-century shoes had the sole and upper joined directly together with a shallow seam (Fig. 72); but by the end of the 12th century it became normal to construct a more watertight seam by stitching a small triangular piece of leather, a rand, between the two main elements (Fig. 73). In the middle of the 15th century the method of construction was altered with the introduction of the turn-welt. It is possible that this originated with the stitching-on of a 'repair' sole, or 'clump' (see below, p. 90 and Fig. 123): not as a true repair but before the shoe was actually worn. Several shoes from Swan Lane (early 15th-century) have soles that are completely untouched, even though a 'clump' has been affixed to them and worn through. From here it would be but a small development to extend the rand and stitch the 'clump' to this, after the shoe had been turned, rather than to the sole or upper (Fig. 74). In this transitional stage tunnel-stitching might still have been used on the outer sole (shown in Fig. 74), as indeed seems proven by at least one 15th-century turn-welt shoe that has recently been recovered from the City of London Boys' School site (excavated in 1986, too late for publication here). Fully-developed turn-welt shoes, however, seem

74 Turn-welt construction. The upper, inner sole and rand have been sewn in the manner shown in Fig. 73, but the rand extends beyond the edge of the shoe and has been used to affix, with tunnel-stitching, a second, outer sole.

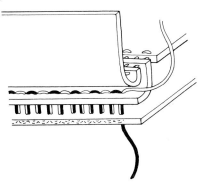

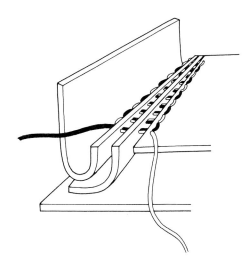

to have had their outer soles attached with grain/flesh stitches, in the manner of the bottom units of composite-soled pattens (see, for example, Thomas 1980, 8 and Fig. 2 No. 57/113/9, probably early 16th-century).

Stitching and seams

The most important seam was that of the lasting-margin, joining the sole to the upper parts (Figs. 72–3). The sole was attached to the lasted upper using an edge/flesh stitch (Figs. 72–3), which meant that there was no exposed stitching on the outer grain surface of the sole, subject to the most wear. Two threads were probably used. Holes would be made with an awl (Fig 71b) and then the threads, whose ends seem to have been attached to a bristle as they are today, would be passed through from opposite sides and pulled tight (*cf.* Fig. 71c and a shoemaker's will of the last quarter of the 15th century (Swann 1986, 5), which lists bristles as part of his kit). It has not been possible to identify the stitching material on the earlier shoes, but on the late 14th-century shoes it was found to be plied, waxed flax (F. Pritchard, pers. comm.). The waxing of the thread made the join more watertight, and also meant that the upper and sole held together, even if only briefly, when the stitching was worn through.

On the earlier shoes, such as those in Figs. 84–5, the upper was attached also using small circular edge/flesh stitches 4 mm apart and 2 mm from the edge of the leather. The shallowness of the seam, coupled with the extreme closeness of the stitches, makes it unlikely that these seams contained a rand (see above). This type of seam occurs on only a few examples, and, since it occurs in the same groups as shoes with the more conventional grain/flesh lasting-margin (*cf.* Fig. 83), should probably be regarded as transitional between the earlier thonged and the later sewn traditions. At this time a grain/flesh lasting-margin also tended to be on the shallow side – *c.*2.5 mm from the edge of the leather with small circular stitches averaging 6 mm apart. A grain/flesh stitch on the upper meant that the seam could be deeper and the threads thicker, factors which also facilitated the inclusion of rands between the upper and the sole. In the 14th-century groups, examples were noted of stitch-holes 3 mm across and 8 mm apart.

The lasting-margin also served to anchor

smaller reinforcement-pieces in place. Triangular pieces of leather were sewn into the heel section, particularly in the higher forms of footwear, to strengthen an area which was subject to great stress and wear. The size and shape of these stiffeners varied tremendously (contrast, for example, Figs. 93, 106 and 107). Whereas the lower edge of the triangle was sewn into the lasting-margin with grain/flesh stitches, the other two sides were anchored to the flesh side of the upper with a shallow binding-stitch which did not penetrate the full thickness of the leather (Fig. 75). The use of this stitch on the heel-stiffener and other reinforcement-pieces, such as lace-hole reinforcements, is evident from the presence of a slightly scalloped edge where the thread has been pulled very tight. Lace-hole reinforcements are occasionally present on the earlier side-laced shoes (Figs. 89–90), and almost invariably on the later ones (Fig. 108). Again, the piece was first stitched into the lasting-margin and then stitched in place on the upper with binding-stitch along both long edges.

A fine, shallow edge/flesh binding-stitch is present on many shoes from the early/mid 12th century onwards along the top edge of the upper. In some cases this may simply have been to reinforce the edge (MacGregor 1982, 140), whereas in others it served to secure a narrow strip of leather or 'topband'. These topbands, which were sometimes single-thickness (Fig. 97) but more often of thin leather folded double (Figs. 89–90, 94), will have given a more finished appearance to

75 Binding-stitch or overstitching, used to attach heel-stiffeners, lace-hole reinforcements, tongues and occasionally top-bands. The stitches do not penetrate the full thickness of the leather and so are invisible on the outside of the shoe.

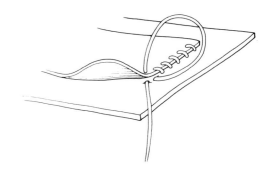

the shoe. A third option, suggested by Richardson (1959, 105), is that such stitching may have been intended to anchor a woven lining in place. Wardrobe accounts throughout the medieval period refer to shoes that were lined, but few such linings survive in archaeological deposits and none from London. A shoe from Perth, however, has been recorded as containing the remains of what may possibly be a lining (Clare Thomas, pers. comm.).

Soles and rand

The sole was normally made of thick cattle leather, placed flesh side up with a loosely-stitched edge/flesh margin around the edge. The soles varied from one to two pieces. Two-piece soles, which were common on large shoes, such as the late 14th-century 'poulaines' (Figs. 102–4), and may have facilitated repairs (see below, p. 89), consisted of a heel and forepart, and were joined at the waist with an edge/flesh butt seam.

The rand was a narrow strip of leather, triangular in section, sewn into the lasting-margin between the sole and upper to make the join more watertight. It began by being cut in several short segments, *c.*4 mm in width, with stitches 1 mm

across and at 7 mm centres, and sometimes seems not to have been used around the entire shoe: one of the 13th-century drawstring boots (Fig. 15), for example, which was recovered absolutely intact from the excavations, has rands at the waist on each side but not around the toe or heel. Later, the rand evolved into longer continuous strips and generally was inserted around the entire circumference of the lasting-margin.

The fashion for long 'poulaines' in the mid and late 14th century posed difficulties for the worker making shoes with the turn-shoe method. Fig. 76 shows the compromise which was achieved for this type of footwear. The shoe was stitched by the normal method until just below the toe section and then stitched off (note the small cluster of stitches on either side). It was then turned right-side out and the sewing continued, possibly from side to side and perhaps using an edge/flesh stitch with a finer thread.

Cutting patterns of uppers

The side seams joining the shoe upper together were also sewn while the shoe was inside out. The shoemakers evidently preferred to use as few main seams, and indeed as few major shoe pieces, as possible. The basic cutting pattern of the early shoes was a one-piece 'wrap-around', with no additions or major modifications to accommodate the fastening, and one major seam at the side, usually the inner side, of the foot. Even when cutting patterns became slightly more complicated with the introduction of the toggle fastening, shoes remained predominantly one-piece wrap-around constructions with inserts. As noted above (p. 43), these side joins were vulnerable, and they were closely and finely stitched using an edge/flesh butt seam (Fig. 77). As with the lasting-margin, two threads were probably used,

76 'Poulaine' sole, showing how the sewing of the shoe had to be modified because of the unusually long narrow shape. It is possible to see on either side, close to the beginning of the 'poulaine' itself, that there are small clusters of stitches as if the thread has been tied off; from this stage on the stitching is smaller and more closely spaced, indicating that the final stitching occured after the rest of the shoe had been sewn and turned right-side out.

77 Edge/flesh butt seam, the most common seam on shoes in the present collection. Used primarily for the main side seams and for the attachment of inserts.

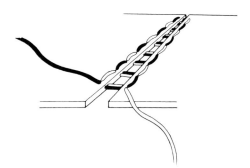

and the holes seem to have been made with an awl. In one instance, a compromise between an overlapped seam (Fig. 78) and a butt seam was achieved by cutting the edges of the leather on an angle (Fig. 79) to obtain a closer fit. These seams were normally used to join the main parts of the upper, but smaller pieces, such as facings (*cf.* Figs. 87, 93) or tongues (*cf.* Figs. 91, 107), were often attached with a binding-seam (Fig. 80). This was done with a single thread, in some cases possibly using a needle rather than an awl and bristle.

Although it was possible to make a drawstring shoe from one piece of leather (Fig. 83), there were exceptions, notably when a miscalculation occurred, or when additional height was required for an ankle-shoe or low boot (*cf.* Figs. 23 and 40). The example shown in Fig. 23 offers a possible explanation for the surprising absence of taller boots (see below, pp. 118–9): additional pieces, such as the one suggested with broken lines, would have a minimum of cut and stitched edges, and could have been easily reused. Fig. 40 shows a low boot based around a one-piece cutting pattern with two inserts to compensate for the extra height. Even with the extra pieces, there are still only three edge/flesh butt seams joining the upper together.

Figs. 89 and 90 represent some of the earliest versions of the side-laced footwear which, with some modifications, was to dominate the early/mid 15th-century groups at Trig Lane (*cf.* Fig. 108). One of them is unusually cut, with both sets of lace-holes in the quarters (Fig. 89). There does not seem to be an obvious advantage in having the lacing on a separate insert (*cf.* Fig. 90), but the use of lace-hole reinforcement-pieces to strengthen the areas of the shoe most subject to wear and weakness was an obvious improvement. Whilst some of the later shoes still show evidence of being based on single-piece cutting patterns (*cf.* Fig. 97), Fig. 108 has a separate vamp and quarters, with a large rectangular insert covering the front of the foot and taking most of the lace-holes down one side. The lace-holes have reinforcement-pieces along their full length, a necessity given their closeness and the tightness with which the boot was evidently laced to fit the wearer's leg.

It is with the 13th-century toggle-fastened shoes that one sees shoemakers beginning to

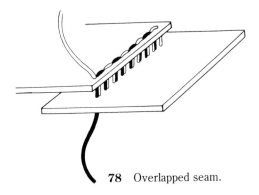

78   Overlapped seam.

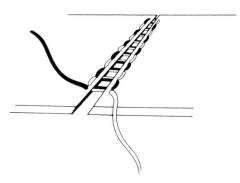

79   Bevelled seam. The edges of the leather have been cut diagonally so that the seam, although shallow, is very close. Found rarely in the present collection, and then only on side seams. Cutting the edges in this way has been common practice from the 18th century onwards, and is generally termed 'skiving'.

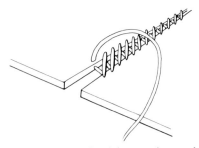

80   Binding-seam, used to join two pieces edge-to-edge. Rarer than the ordinary butt seam, this was generally used only for small inserts or edgings. It is easily recognised by the edge/flesh stitches on both pieces and by the deep scalloped impressions caused by the thread having been whipped across and pulled tight.

plan, cut and stitch items of footwear with large deliberate (as opposed to random) inserts to take either toggles or 'buttonholes' (Figs. 91–2). The main side seam remained a butt seam, but the insert was anchored in place with binding-stitch. A further innovation was the attachment of what seems to have been a reinforcement cord to strengthen the edges. This is marked by a broad, deep channel straddled by tunnel-stitches, and a shoe from 'Baynards Castle', on which the thread survives partially intact, supports the reconstruction proposed in Fig. 81. On toggle-fastened shoes a thick thread or cord of this type was often stitched just inside the outer edge of the 'buttonholes' and down along the V-shaped cut at the instep, which presumably allowed more flexibility as the shoe was being put on (Fig. 92). It was only in the mid to late 14th century that the one-piece cutting pattern was abandoned in favour of a two-piece shoe, consisting of a vamp and separate quarters. These had two main low-cut butt seams on either side of the foot with the vulnerable latchet or buckle straps held in place with a butt seam and reinforcment cord (Figs. 102–4).

81 Shallow binding-stitch used to anchor reinforcement cords. Occurs particularly on mid to late 14th-century low-cut shoes, along the vamp throat, on the fastening straps and along the upper edges of the quarters.

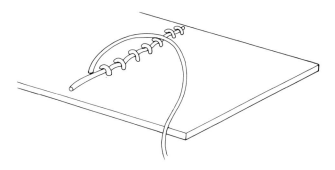

82 Shoe or ankle-shoe (early/mid 12th-century). A row of tunnel-stitches inset from the edge, rather than edge/flesh stitches along the edge itself, was used to join the sole to the upper. The upper was probably made entirely in one piece, although binding-stitch marks the position of a flap, insert or top-band at the vamp throat. The main seam (butt-stitched) is on the inner side. Slots, no doubt once on both sides, will have held a thong – or pair of interwoven thongs – which were both decorative and a means of shaping the upper around the foot. Scale 1:3.

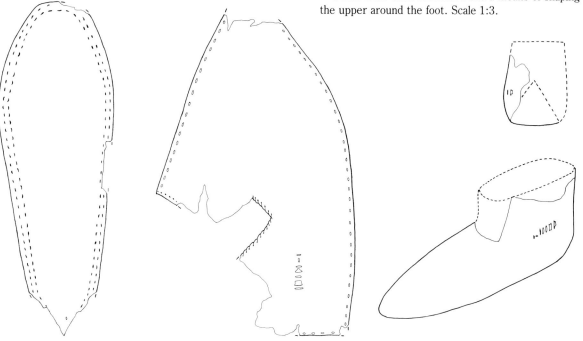

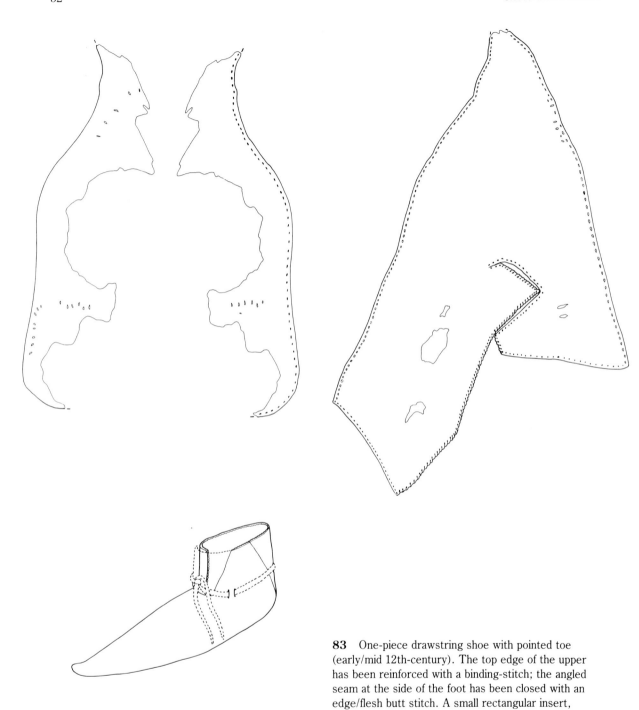

83 One-piece drawstring shoe with pointed toe
(early/mid 12th-century). The top edge of the upper
has been reinforced with a binding-stitch; the angled
seam at the side of the foot has been closed with an
edge/flesh butt stitch. A small rectangular insert,
stitched with an edge/flesh butt seam, would have
closed the throat area. The sole (lower, grain side,
left; upper, flesh side, *right*) is virtually straight-sided;
stitch-holes show that it was repaired. Scale 1:3.

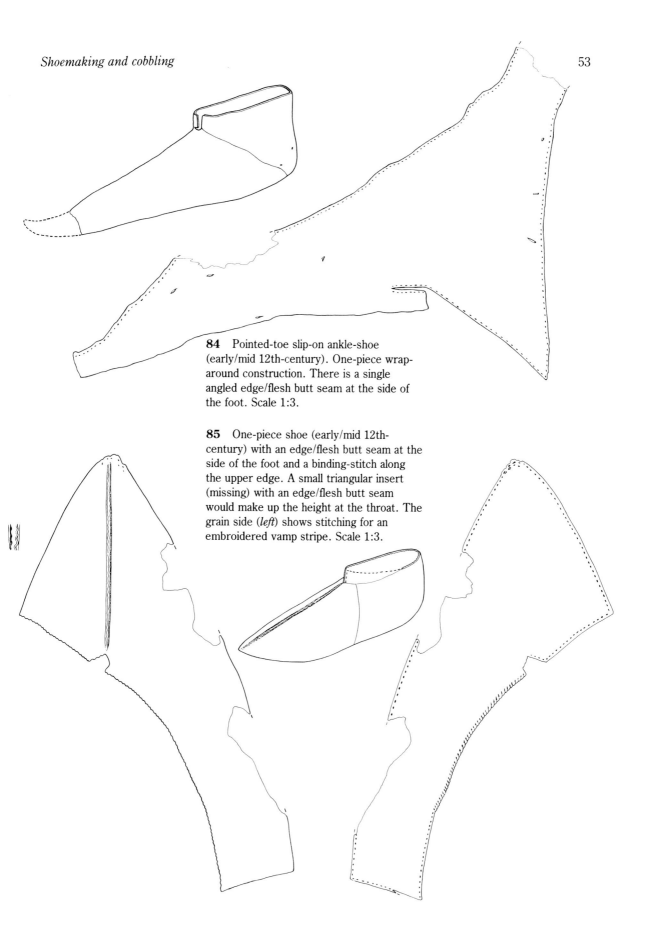

84 Pointed-toe slip-on ankle-shoe (early/mid 12th-century). One-piece wrap-around construction. There is a single angled edge/flesh butt seam at the side of the foot. Scale 1:3.

85 One-piece shoe (early/mid 12th-century) with an edge/flesh butt seam at the side of the foot and a binding-stitch along the upper edge. A small triangular insert (missing) with an edge/flesh butt seam would make up the height at the throat. The grain side (*left*) shows stitching for an embroidered vamp stripe. Scale 1:3.

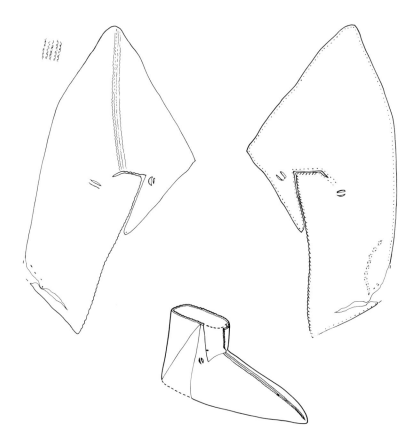

86   Main part of a drawstring ankle-shoe (early/mid 12th-century), with a binding-stitch along the upper edge and edge/flesh butt seams at the side of the foot. The shoe originally had two inserts – a triangular insert at the side of the foot, and a small rectangular insert at the throat held in place by an edge/flesh butt seam. Tunnel-stitching marks the position of a semicircular heel-stiffener (missing). The grain side (*left*) shows an embroidered vamp stripe. Scale 1:3.

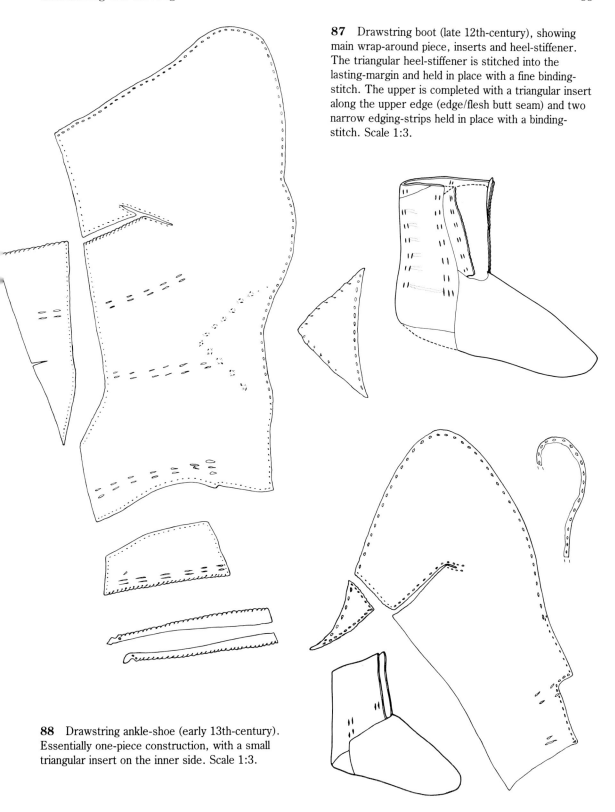

87 Drawstring boot (late 12th-century), showing main wrap-around piece, inserts and heel-stiffener. The triangular heel-stiffener is stitched into the lasting-margin and held in place with a fine binding-stitch. The upper is completed with a triangular insert along the upper edge (edge/flesh butt seam) and two narrow edging-strips held in place with a binding-stitch. Scale 1:3.

88 Drawstring ankle-shoe (early 13th-century). Essentially one-piece construction, with a small triangular insert on the inner side. Scale 1:3.

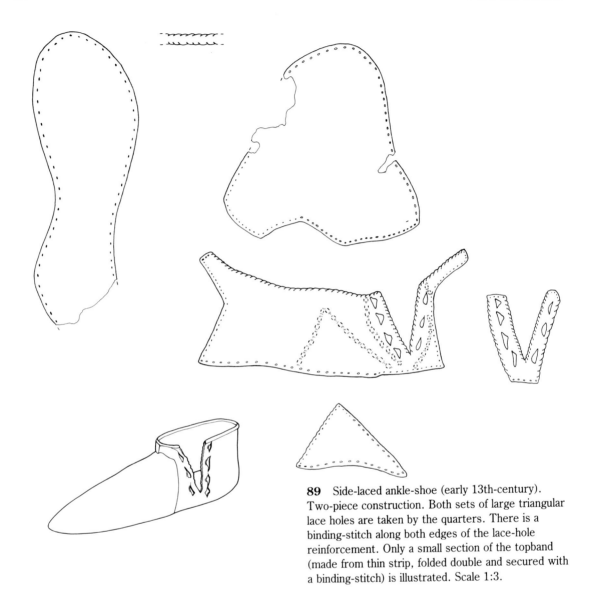

89 Side-laced ankle-shoe (early 13th-century).
Two-piece construction. Both sets of large triangular
lace holes are taken by the quarters. There is a
binding-stitch along both edges of the lace-hole
reinforcement. Only a small section of the topband
(made from thin strip, folded double and secured with
a binding-stitch) is illustrated. Scale 1:3.

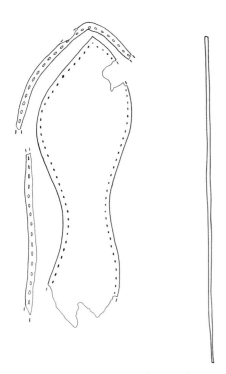

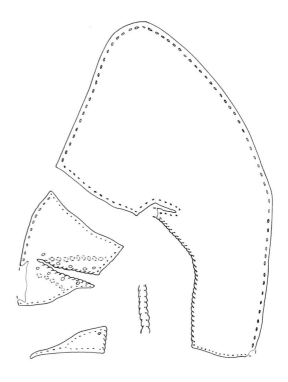

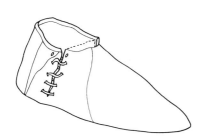

90 Side-laced ankle-shoe (early 13th-century). Although contemporary with Fig. 89 and of the same basic style, this shoe is one-piece with the lace holes on a separate insert. They were punched out and threaded with a single continuous lace. Again only part of the topband is illustrated. Scale 1:3.

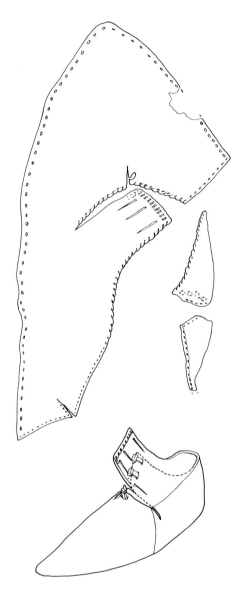

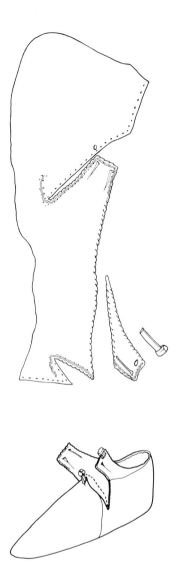

91 Toggle-fastened low ankle-shoe (mid 13th-century). The main piece is seamed at the instep with a binding-seam, and a triangular tongue, itself in two parts, was stitched along it. A rectangular insert with a 'buttonhole' and two toggles (cf. Fig. 92) is missing from the opposing vamp wing. Scale 1:3.

92 Toggle-fastened low ankle-shoe (late 13th-century). Note the reinforcement cord stitched along the edge of the quarters and the V-cut in the pattern to ease putting the shoe on. Scale 1:3.

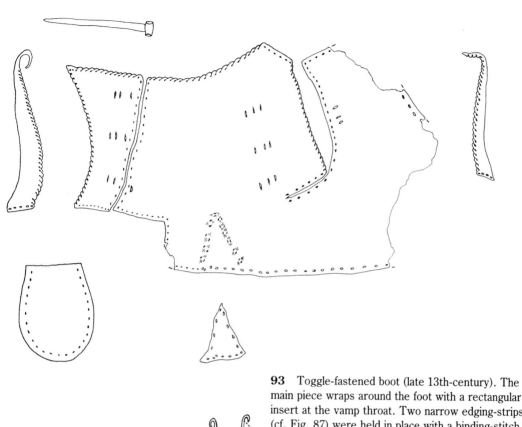

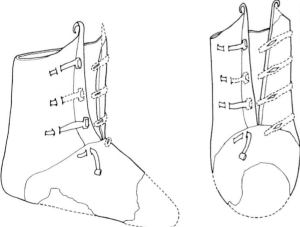

93 Toggle-fastened boot (late 13th-century). The main piece wraps around the foot with a rectangular insert at the vamp throat. Two narrow edging-strips (cf. Fig. 87) were held in place with a binding-stitch. The small heel-stiffener was also sewn along two edges with a binding-stitch. Scale 1:3.

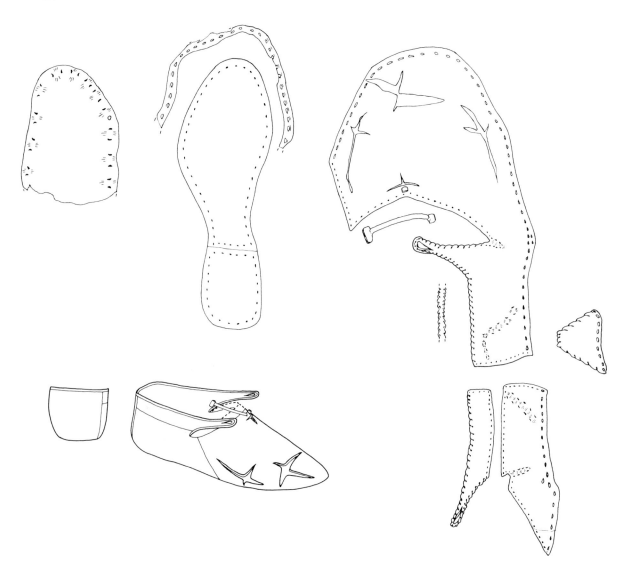

94 Toggle-fastened shoe (mid 14th-century). This
is still based on a single main piece, but there is an
additional component ('quarter') extending from the
back of the heel to the side of the foot. The vertical
seam at the heel is an edge/flesh butt seam, further
strengthened by the oversewing of a heel-stiffener.
The edges have been sewn with a binding-stitch and
the topband, which would have been attached to
them, survives in full (only a small section illustrated).
A long triangular tongue, which would have been
sewn along the full length of the vamp throat (cf.
Fig. 91) is missing. Note the repair piece for the sole
and the widely-spaced tunnel-stitches. Scale 1:3.

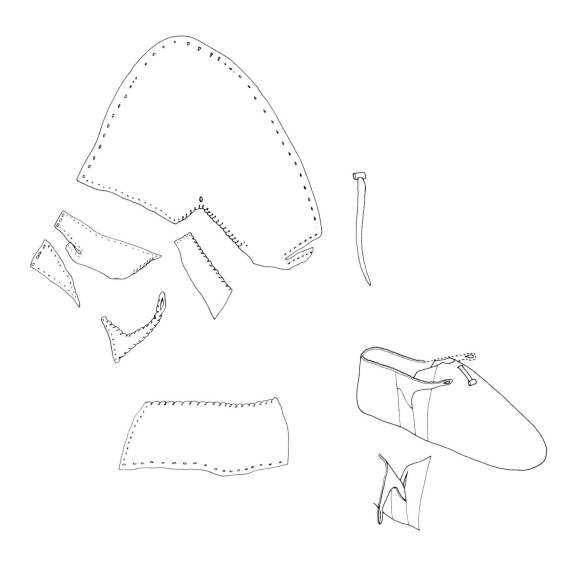

95 Toggle-fastened shoe (mid 14th-century), made with separate vamp and quarters. On the inner side are a series of inserts arranged to ease putting the shoe on the foot and to take one of the two straps; the construction of the outer side will have been similar, but since the quarters have been cut back the details are unknown. All the vulnerable upper edges have been overstitched with a binding-stitch, probably for a topband. The tongue was made in two parts (one part only surviving), which were joined with a central butt seam; it was fastened to the vamp throat with a binding-seam. Scale 1:3.

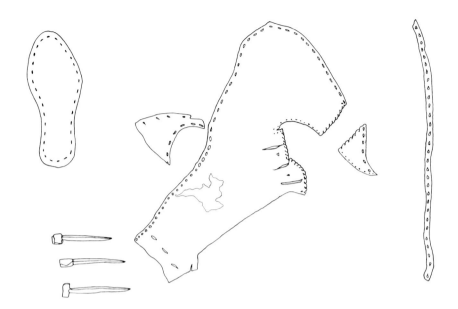

96 Child's toggle-fastened boot (mid 14th-century). The main piece wraps around the foot, with a diagonal edge/flesh butt seam. There is a small triangular insert at the lasting-margin to fill the gap left by the main piece. The boot had a single-piece sole. Note the continuous strip of rand. Scale 1:3.

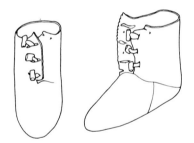

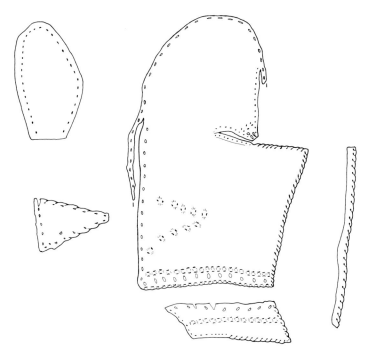

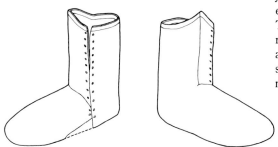

97 Side-laced boot (mid 14th-century). The main wrap-around piece and the rectangular insert were joined vertically at the instep, partly with an edge/flesh butt seam and partly with a binding-seam. The lace holes were originally strengthened with a reinforcement piece (missing), which was anchored along both edges with binding-stitches. The topband survives, but a small triangular insert at the lasting-margin is now missing. Scale 1:3.

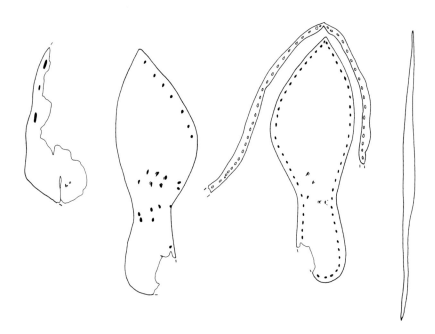

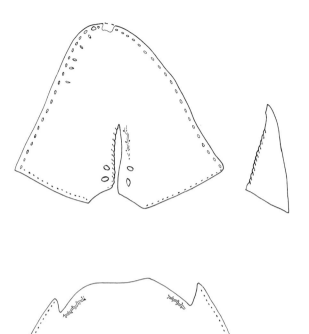

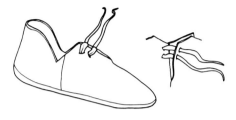

98   Front-laced shoe (mid 14th-century), made in two parts. Contrast the shape of the quarters with that of earlier two-piece shoes, such as Fig. 95, which were cut straight across the back of the heel; here they are high at the back and dip low at either side. The shoe had a single lace and a tongue attached with a binding-seam to only one side of the vamp opening. The repair sole survives in part. Scale 1:3.

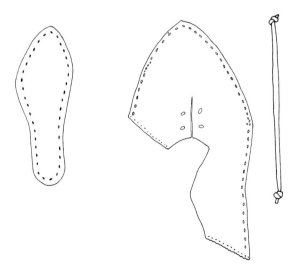

99   Front-laced one-piece shoe (late 14th-century). There are no reinforcement stitches around the lace holes. Although the quarters and vamp are one continuous piece of leather, the quarters retain the high profile at the heel which was noted on the previous two-piece shoe (Fig. 98). Scale 1:3.

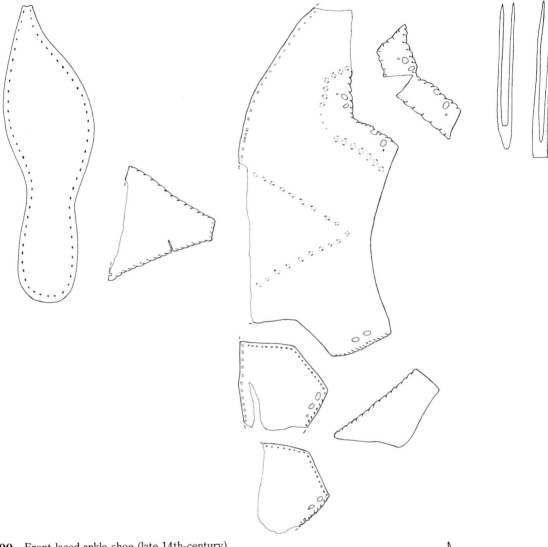

100 Front-laced ankle-shoe (late 14th-century).
The upper was originally made in one piece (for a
similar cutting-pattern see Fig. 106), but since the toe
has been destroyed it is now broken into two. The
large reinforcement patch on the inner side is
unusual: the butt-stitched seam shows that it could
not have been added *after* the shoe was lasted (as the
reinforcement on the outer side probably was) but
that it was included when the main seam of the shoe
was being sewn – either as an intentional part of the
original construction or as a major repair. The tongue
was sewn edge-to-edge with binding-stitch on the
inner side only. Note the pair of bifurcated, latchet-
type laces. Scale 1:3.

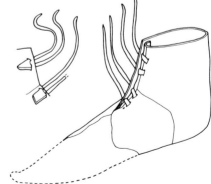

101 Front-laced ankle-shoe (late 14th-century). There is one main piece, but a small insert (now missing) was sewn in, partly with binding-stitches, partly with butt stitches, to make up the height on the inner vamp wing. The heel-stiffener is also missing. Impressions around the edges of the vamp throat suggest the former presence of a reinforcement cord, rather than a tongue. Scale 1:3.

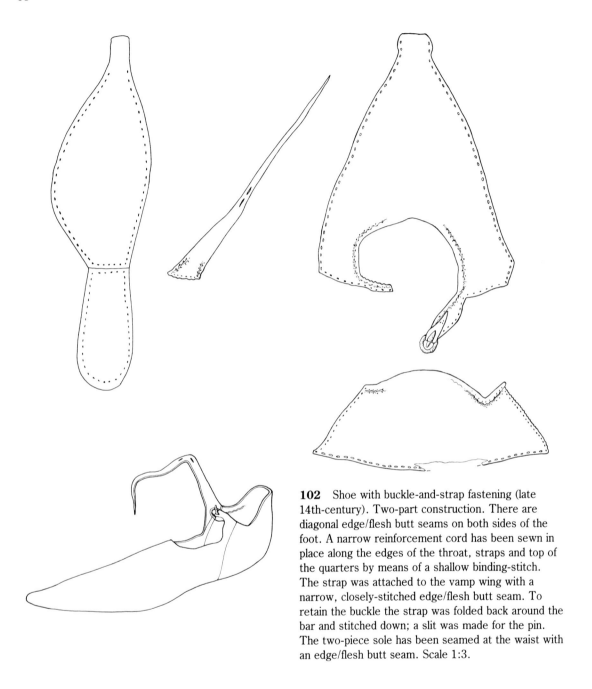

102 Shoe with buckle-and-strap fastening (late 14th-century). Two-part construction. There are diagonal edge/flesh butt seams on both sides of the foot. A narrow reinforcement cord has been sewn in place along the edges of the throat, straps and top of the quarters by means of a shallow binding-stitch. The strap was attached to the vamp wing with a narrow, closely-stitched edge/flesh butt seam. To retain the buckle the strap was folded back around the bar and stitched down; a slit was made for the pin. The two-piece sole has been seamed at the waist with an edge/flesh butt seam. Scale 1:3.

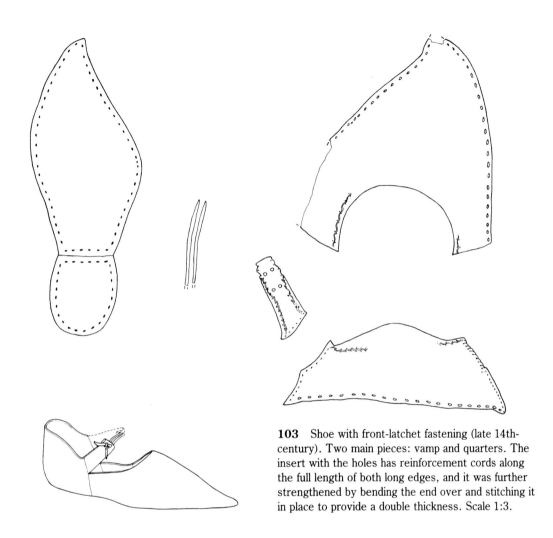

103 Shoe with front-latchet fastening (late 14th-century). Two main pieces: vamp and quarters. The insert with the holes has reinforcement cords along the full length of both long edges, and it was further strengthened by bending the end over and stitching it in place to provide a double thickness. Scale 1:3.

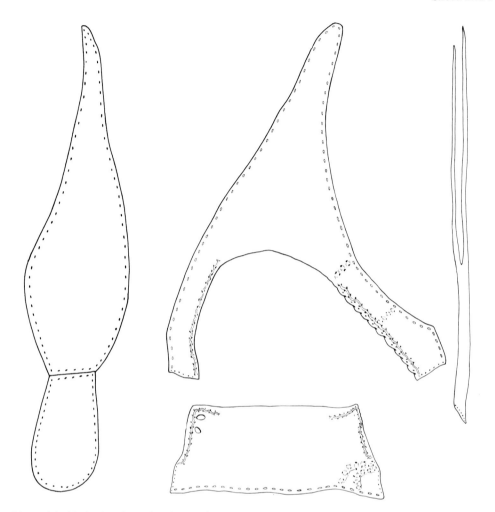

104 Shoe with side-latchet fastening (late 14th-century). The holes are taken by the quarters and reinforced with a cord. The latchet was originally held in place with an edge/flesh butt-seam. On the inner side are rows of stitch-holes and, along the upper edge, the remains of a binding-seam which mark the former presence of two rectangular patches; these were probably added successively and, because they clearly pass over the reinforcement cord, may not have been an original part of the shoe. They may have been stitched in to strengthen the side seam – perhaps after the shoe had split apart. Scale 1:3.

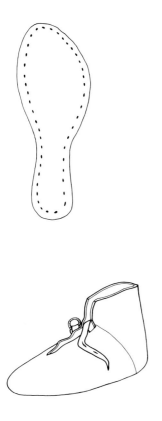

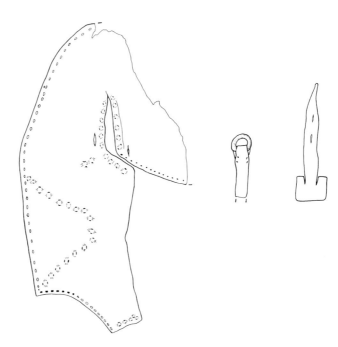

105 One-piece ankle-shoe (early 15th-century) closed with a buckle and strap. Tunnel-stitches show the position of the heel-stiffener and tongue; impressions suggest that the latter was sewn along one edge only, while a reinforcement cord ran along the other. One of the straps has a large spade-shaped terminal to prevent it slipping through the slit, but tunnel-stitching suggests that the other strap was sewn down on the inside. Scale 1:3.

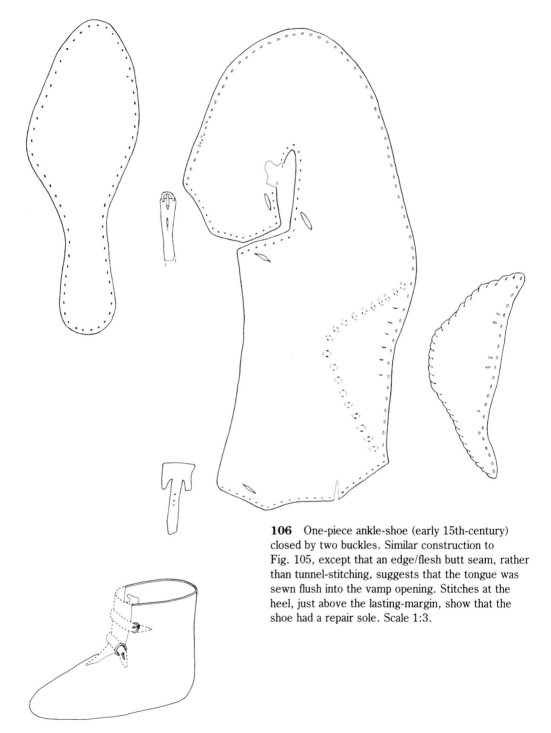

106 One-piece ankle-shoe (early 15th-century) closed by two buckles. Similar construction to Fig. 105, except that an edge/flesh butt seam, rather than tunnel-stitching, suggests that the tongue was sewn flush into the vamp opening. Stitches at the heel, just above the lasting-margin, show that the shoe had a repair sole. Scale 1:3.

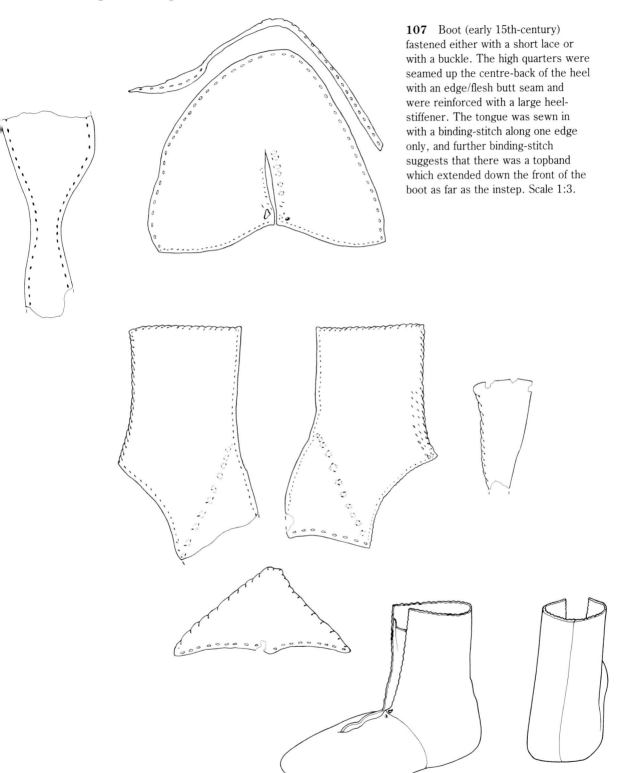

107 Boot (early 15th-century) fastened either with a short lace or with a buckle. The high quarters were seamed up the centre-back of the heel with an edge/flesh butt seam and were reinforced with a large heel-stiffener. The tongue was sewn in with a binding-stitch along one edge only, and further binding-stitch suggests that there was a topband which extended down the front of the boot as far as the instep. Scale 1:3.

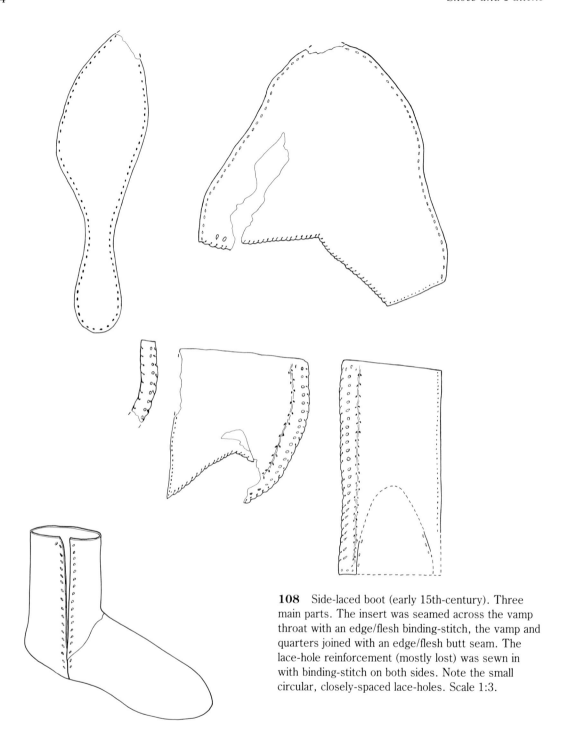

108 Side-laced boot (early 15th-century). Three
main parts. The insert was seamed across the vamp
throat with an edge/flesh binding-stitch, the vamp and
quarters joined with an edge/flesh butt seam. The
lace-hole reinforcement (mostly lost) was sewn in
with binding-stitch on both sides. Note the small
circular, closely-spaced lace-holes. Scale 1:3.

Buckles and strap ends

June Swann (1981) traces the importance of the shoe buckle as a fashion accessory to 1660 and Pepys's entry in his diary that 'This day I began to put on buckles to my shoes' (22nd January, 1660; ed. Latham & Matthews 1970–83, i.26). The buckles of the 17th century far exceeded their medieval counterparts in elaboration, perhaps partly as a reaction to the austerity of the Puritan Commonwealth, but this is not to say that medieval shoe buckles were not intended to be decorative, as the buckles in Fig. 110, especially Nos. d to f, will show. Chemical spot-tests (by Helen Ganiaris, Museum of London Conservation Laboratory) indicate that all the late 14th-century buckles are of iron, with 8 of the 19 bearing traces of tinning (Table 14). The remaining 11 may have been tinned originally: the plating may have worn away in use, been destroyed by corrosion or simply not detected by the analytical techniques that were used. Iron buckles with traces of tinning were also found in the 15th-century groups (6 in all). There is also one copper-alloy buckle, but at this period by far the majority seem to have been of lead alloy with iron pins (25 examples). Almost invariably the buckle was slipped through a strap, after which one end of the strap was passed through a slit in itself to create a secure loop (Fig. 109).

There are only two strap ends in the present collection, and both were associated with early/mid 15th-century buckled shoes. They are very similar. The one illustrated in Fig. 110j consists of an undecorated rectangular piece of tinned iron, folded over the still-surviving leather strap and held in place with a single rivet; the other end of the strap will have passed through a slit (*cf.* Figs. 105–6) and been sewn down on the inside of the shoe.

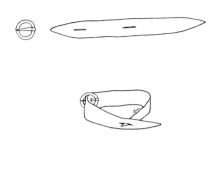

109 The method used to attach a buckle to its strap.

Decoration

Embroidery (by Frances Pritchard)

The collection contains nearly 30 shoes that were once decorated with embroidery – a high total that is commensurate with the impression gained from historical and pictorial, as well as archaeological, sources of the popularity of embroidered shoes, of various types, throughout early medieval Europe. Many shoes documented as being embellished with embroidery had uppers of samite, a twilled silk cloth. This is substantiated by surviving examples, among which are those of two archbishops of Canterbury, Hubert Walter (d. 1205) and Edmund Rich (d. 1241) (Christie 1938, Cat. Nos. 16 and 29). The style of embroidery is that termed *opus anglicanum* with birds, beasts, flowers, foliage scrolls, stars and moons worked in gold and silk thread. Leather shoes were also lavishly embellished on the Continent but less

Table 14. Metal analysis of all buckles in the collection that are still attached to shoes.

	Iron	Tinned iron	Lead alloy with iron pin	Copper alloy	Total
'Baynards Castle' (late 14th c.)	11	8	—	—	19
Swan Lane (early/mid 15th c.)	—	2	6	—	8
Trig Lane (early/mid 15th c.)	—	4	19	1	24
Total	11	14	25	1	51

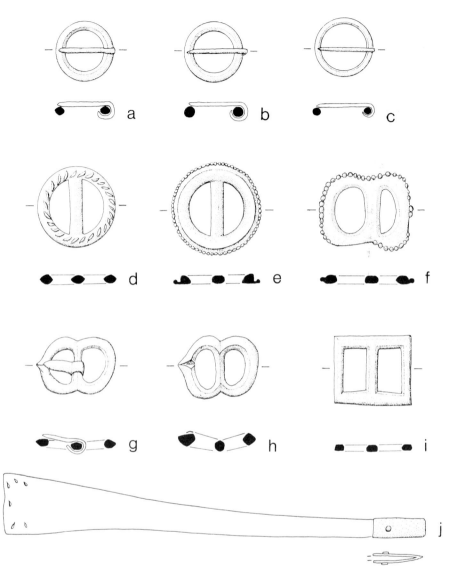

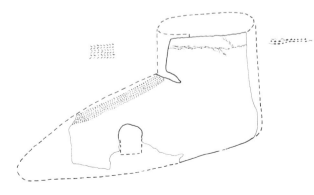

110 Early/mid 15th-century shoe buckles and strap end. Lead/tin alloy with iron pin (a, b, d–g); tinned iron (c, j); copper alloy (i). Scale 1:1.

111 Embroidered decoration. Mid/late 12th-century ankle-shoe decorated with a vamp stripe and an elaborate border on the quarters just below the ankle. Scale 1:3 approx.

emphasis was placed on embroidery alone and in the 12th century it was often combined with appliqué work using gilded strips of leather. Pontifical shoes from tombs in Lausanne and Delémont in Switzerland and Castel St Elia in central Italy illustrate this technique, with chain stitching in silk thread being used to outline the gilded ornament (Schmedding 1978, 100–101; Braun 1899, 293, Abb. 1).

Information concerning embroidered leather shoes worn in England can now be gained from excavated material, which thus encompasses footwear from lower down the social scale. It appears from these that the most common form of embroidered decoration was the vamp stripe extending from the tip of the toe to the throat, which reached the peak of its popularity during the first half of the 12th century. The only other embroidery on a shoe from London is a line sewn immediately below the heel opening of an ankle-shoe from Swan Lane, which is also exceptional in having a peep-hole cut in the vamp (Fig. 111).

Three methods of making the stripes are apparent from the twenty-eight London examples. The earliest occurs on a round-toed shoe from Swan Lane where the upper was joined to the sole with a strip of leather rather than with animal hair or linen thread, thus suggesting that it dates from the 10th or early 11th century (Fig. 112c). The same technique was followed on a late 11th- or early 12th-century ankle-shoe with a more pointed toe from Billingsgate (Fig. 112d). An awl with a small, S-shaped blade was used to incise the grain face of the leather either while the shoe was still in pieces or after it had been turned. On the Billingsgate ankle-shoe there are two rows of such holes, showing that the decoration was limited to a single stripe, while four rows of incisions for two stripes spaced 3 mm apart are present on the shoe from Swan Lane. A decorative thread was next sewn from side to side passing through the holes, but regrettably none of the thread is preserved to indicate the pattern or type of stitching.

A similar method of decoration is to be seen on two 'Carolingian' shoes from the abbey at Middleburg on the island of Walcheren, with one having diagonal stripes along the wing as well as down the centre of the vamp (Hendriks 1964, 112–115). The supposed 9th-century date of these shoes, and the presence of footwear with similar vamp stripes at Elisenhof, Hedeby and Lund hints at a possible Continental influence behind this style.

A second method, represented by a fragmentary ankle-shoe of late 11th- or early 12th-century date from Billingsgate, was more intricate (Fig. 112a–b). The vamp was slit down the centre below the edge of the throat. Tiny slots were subsequently cut, penetrating the flesh as well as the grain of the leather, through which a thread was drawn. The throat end of the seam was strengthened by sewing both edges together while the shoe was still inside out, grain/flesh stitch holes on one edge matching pairs of tunnel-stitches on the other. The nearest parallels to this vamp seam occur on one-piece shoes from Lembecksburg and Lottorf Mose in north Germany, where the design of the shoe was such that the vamp was left open at each end and had to be seamed down the centre (Hald 1972, 71–75, Figs. 75, 76, 79 and 80). The vamp stripe can thus be traced to a constructional feature which lingered on as a decorative device, although on the basis of associated red-painted, Pingsdorf pottery the Lembecksburg shoe probably dates to only a few years earlier than the shoe from Billingsgate.

The last method to evolve and the most common among those from London was to sew the thread directly through the grain of the leather without first marking out the position of the stitches, although scorelines do occur on all four of the shoes with single stripes from late 12th-century deposits (Fig. 112e–g). As a consequence, the stitching became more finely spaced, with up to eleven holes per 10 mm compared with three holes per 10 mm for the earliest technique described. Three shoes in this group retain traces of sewing thread along the vamp and on two of them some of the stitches remain intact. These stripes show that single-stranded silk thread was used for the embroidery, which would have slipped smoothly through the leather without causing undue strain and would have glimmered more lustrously than a twisted or plied thread. The stitch employed, plait-stitch (Fig. 113), was also well suited to embellishing leather since most of the thread remains visible on the surface while the reverse consists of hidden rows of horizontal tunnel-stitches. The stripes were embroidered in different coloured silks, the best-preserved example, from Seal House, having three stripes of contrasting red, white and (faded) green (Fig.

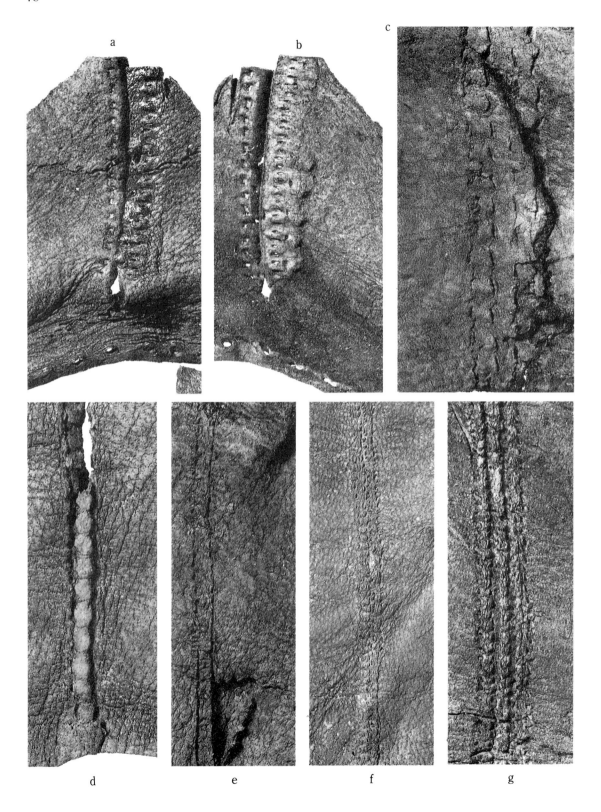

112 Embroidered decoration. *a*: Detail of vamp seam on a late 11th/early 12th-century ankle-shoe. The left edge overlapped the right and was sewn down the centre with a running-stitch. The edge of the leather was skived to make the seam lie smooth. Grain side. *b*: The same vamp seam seen from the flesh side. Five tunnel-stitches reinforced the start of the seam. *c*: Detail of vamp stripe, marked by four lines of incisions, on a 10th- or 11th-century round-toed shoe. *d*: Detail of vamp stripe, marked by two lines of incisions, on a late 11th/early 12th-century ankle-shoe. The large size of the stitch impressions may be contrasted with (*g*). *e–g*: Vamp stripes composed of two, four and six lines of stitch-holes on 12th-century ankle-shoes. The position of the single stripe was lightly scored before being sewn. Scale 2:1.

---

114); another, from Swan Lane, has red and white stripes. A comparative group of 12th-century shoes from Bergen, Norway has a number of more elaborately-embroidered shoes and these show that different blocks of colour were sometimes present along a single stripe (Inger R. Pedersen and Arne Larsen, pers. comm.). The repertoire of stitches also embraced cross-stitch and satin-stitch. Thus the full range of patterns on the London shoes can only be conjectured in view of the decay of most of the embroidery thread.

The technique of plait-stitch falls into a category of embroidery known as canvas work, sometimes called *opus pulvinarium* in the 13th century because it was a popular means of decorating cushions (Christie 1938, 83). A cushion from the grave of archbishop Walter de Gray (d. 1255), who was a regent of England during the minority of Henry III, was couched in gold thread on a ground worked in plait-stitch and cross-stitch (King 1971, 129), while the pattern of the cushion from the spectacular tomb of Fernando de la Cerda (d. 1275), in the mausoleum of the Castilian royal family at the convent of Las Huelgas in Burgos, was worked entirely in plait-stitch (Gómez-Moreno 1946, 86, Pls. cxxiii–cxxiv). The stole of archbishop Hubert Walter is an earlier embroidery in plait-stitch but like the de Gray cushion it is in a fragmentary condition since the 'canvas'-like material used for the foundation has rotted away beneath the embroidery stitches (Christie 1938, 59, Cat. No. 18). The London shoes made from leather, a more resilient material

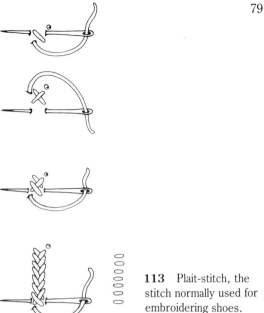

113 Plait-stitch, the stitch normally used for embroidering shoes.

than canvas, thus enable a gap to be filled in the historical record of this form of embroidery, indicating that it was flourishing on a considerable scale in the 12th century as well as in succeeding years. The wide extent of the practice can perhaps be gauged by the fact that similar embroidered shoes, albeit mainly lacking in any sewing thread, have been excavated in England in Durham, York, Lincoln, Coventry, Oxford, Worcester, Gloucester and Winchester.

Openwork

After embroidered vamp stripes, this is the most common form of decoration on the shoes in the collection. All the uppers with this sort of decoration may be seen in Figs. 115–117. The decoration seems to have been effected after the shoe pieces had been cut out and before the shoe was stitched together. The work seems to have been done freehand, without the assistance of guide-lines but possibly with some sort of cutting pattern. Although sometimes the designs could be combined with great skill and effect, mostly the stamps were impressed in straight lines, carefully spaced to minimise the possibility of tears between one opening and the next.

The earliest example, Fig. 115a, dates to the first half of the 13th century. Compared with later examples, the work seems very cautious, with a variety of 4 small motifs averaging 8 by 2 mm

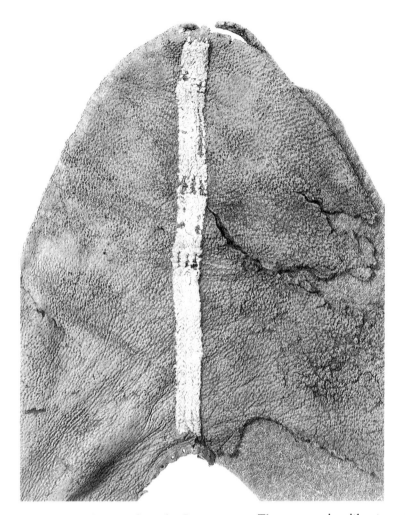

114 Embroidered
decoration. Detail of vamp
stripe on an early/mid 12th-
century ankle-shoe. The
three rows were embroidered
in plait-stitch using red, white
and green silk. The stripes
were not always sewn in the
same direction: here, the two
lines on the left were stitched
from the vamp throat to the
toe and the one on the right
from the toe to the throat.
Scale 1:1.

maximum and approximately 5 mm apart. The
decoration continues as far as 15–16 mm from the
lasting-margin, with the probable effect that the
shoe when sewn would have been covered by
decoration on all its visible surfaces.

The surface of Fig. 116b, probably late 14th-
century in date, is covered with diamond-shaped
openings with wavy serrated edges, the whole
effect being similar to the lattice-work decoration
which occurs frequently in manuscript illustrations, and which could be embroidered, cut out or
incised (*cf.* below Figs. 119a and 120, and one
vamp in the Museum of London collection (MOL
4674) which actually combines openwork with
engraved lattice-work). The corners of the pattern have been filled out with triangular openings
so that the pattern is finished off at the lasting-

margin without any irregular edges. The openings
are larger and the spacing is closer than on the
early/mid 13th-century shoe, indicating that the
style was slightly more developed at this stage and
that the shoemakers were more familiar with the
limitations imposed by this type of decoration.

Fig. 116a shows what happens to the shoe
upper when the motifs are both too large and too
closely spaced. The smaller motifs, which are
more widely spaced, hold the shape of the intended pattern better. The size of the openings
has allowed the leather to stretch and distort here.

The shoe in Fig. 115c has survived as the
quarters only, this time decorated with elongated
motifs placed horizontally. The stamps have been
lined up in columns and staggered, so that the
whole surface is covered. A couple of stamps have

been placed vertically at the narrow edges to fill
the space more evenly. As in the other examples,
there is no indication of the use of guidelines. The
shoes in Figs. 117a–b only have openwork
decoration enhancing their low-cut vamp throats.
Fig. 117a has two concentric rows of oval perforations, whilst 117b has four pairs of long narrow
slits.

The last example in this section (Fig. 116c) is
also the finest, and is reminiscent of the fine openwork decoration on the shoes depicted in a painting from St. Stephen's Chapel, Westminster (Fig.
118). The pattern is both complicated and fragile.
The surface of the vamp is divided into narrower
and wider panels by the different motifs and com-
binations of motifs. The widest rows are formed
by serrated lozenges edged with plain triangular
stamps. Beside these are narrow transverse rows
of small crosses, as well as wider panels of alternating triangles. The stamps have been carefully
and closely spaced – 4 mm apart – but it is probable that the alternating narrow rows of smaller
stamps help the wider panels retain their shape.

115 Openwork decoration. *a*: Vamp and quarters of
side-laced shoe (early 13th-century; for reconstruction
see Fig. 25). Flesh side (inside) shown. The insert to
take the opposing lace holes is missing. There are
diagonal edge/flesh butt seams on either side of the
foot. *b*: Fragment of vamp (mid/late 14th-century).
Grain side (outside). *c*: Quarters of buckle- or latchet-
fastened shoe (late 14th-century). Grain side. Scale
1:3.

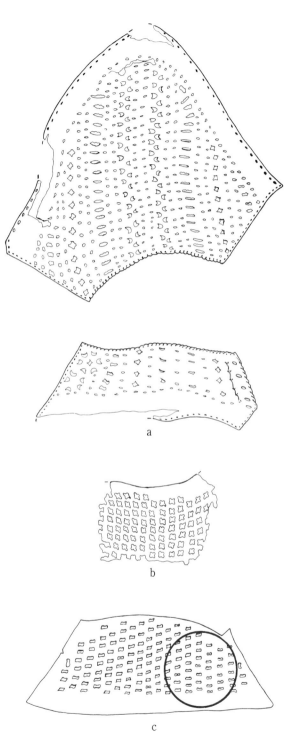

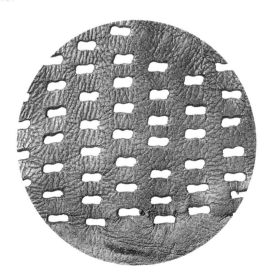

116 Openwork decoration. *a, b*: Vamp fragments
from side-laced ankle-shoes or boots (not stratified,
but probably late 14th/early 15th-century). *c*: Vamp
fragment from shoe of unknown type (early/mid 15th-
century). Scale 1:3.

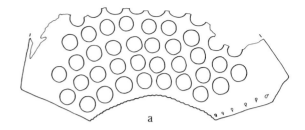

a

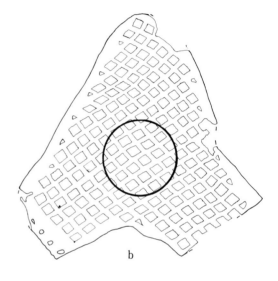

b

c

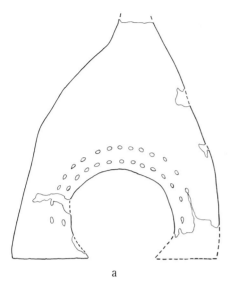

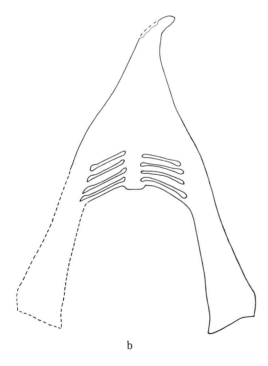

a

b

117 Openwork decoration. *a, b*: Vamps of buckle- or latchet-fastened shoes (late 14th-century). Scale 1:3.

The fragility of such work is attested by the survival of this vamp in several pieces with some of the leather torn between one opening and the next.

Incised and engraved

Fig. 119a, datable to the late 14th-century, is covered with shallowly-*incised*, closely-spaced lattice-work. The panels of incised decoration are separated by plain strips edged by narrow lines where the leather surface has been scraped back to provide a contrasting felted (suede-like) effect. The same treatment has been given to the outline of the design just inside the lasting-margin.

There are several points of interest to be noted about this mode of decoration. The first is the use of shallow incision with a sharp instrument, as opposed to the engraved decoration (with a blunt instrument) which was so popular on other forms of leatherwork (Cowgill, de Neergaard & Griffiths 1987, 40 and 43). The incised work which has been recorded on leather scabbards of the same period is fairly crude in relation to the work on this shoe, although it will be noted that the lines used, except the edging, are all straight, since curved lines were difficult to incise with any degree of precision and accuracy. The leather used for shoe uppers is much thinner than that used for scabbards, and thus required a greater degree of precision to avoid cutting through the entire thickness. However, shoes in the present collection which are decorated in this way all date to the late 14th century, the time when incised decoration was most popular (Russell 1939, 139).

The second point of interest is the scraping back of the grain side of the leather to create a different surface effect. The same effect has been noted on scabbards from 'Baynards Castle' of a slightly earlier date – i.e. mid, as opposed to late, 14th-century (Cowgill, de Neergaard & Griffiths 1987, 41) – but it was not possible in those instances to determine whether the tonal difference was in fact the result of scraping back the surface, or of impressing a hot implement briefly on the leather. It is possible on this shoe actually to see the knife marks where the leather has been pared away (Fig. 119a detail). It seems likely that the areas to be decorated were marked out with a shallow incision, prior to the deeper incision of the lattice. After this, the wider edging strips were cut back

118   Detail of painting (now lost) from St. Stephen's
Chapel, Westminster, showing shoes with elaborate
openwork decoration.

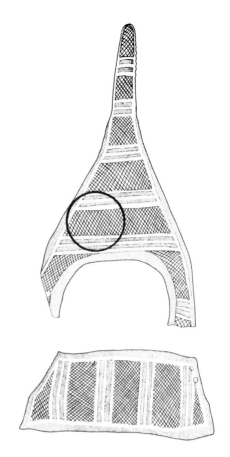

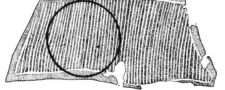

119 Incised and scraped decoration. *a*: Vamp and quarters of side-latchet shoe (late 14th-century; for reconstruction see Fig. 51). *b*: Quarters, probably of side-latchet shoe (late 14th-century). Scale 1:3.

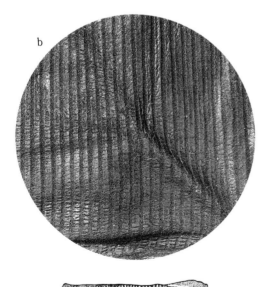

so that any overcutting of the lattice could be removed.

In contrast with the above shoe, the shoe in Fig. 121c has been decorated with *engraving*. The lines are shallower and wider and have been affected by pressure on the leather rather than by the sharpness of the cutting edge. There is a central triangular decorative panel filled with a three-leaved motif; this is edged by two plain lines and by three lines where the leather has been stripped back as described above. The spaces at each side have been decorated with continuous rows of leaves engraved along the sloping lines, with finely engraved parallel lines serving as a filler for the remaining empty space (see Fig. 121c detail). The overall effect is one of symmetry, with the design carefully worked out to fit the required piece of leather. The leaf motifs, which occur on a number of shoe fragments in this group, seem to be variations of the vine or ivy scrolls popular on other forms of leatherwork during the late medieval period. Again it seems most likely, given the structure of the design, that the areas to be decorated were marked out beforehand with shallow engraved lines.

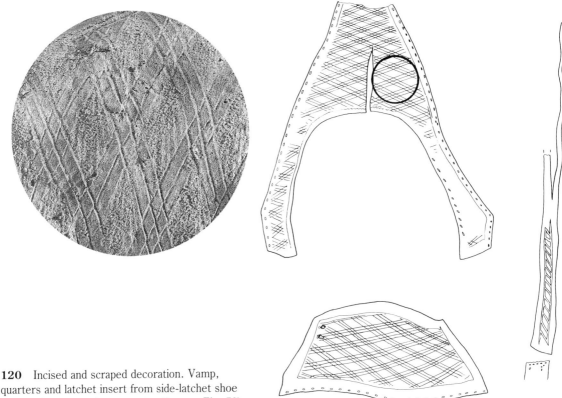

120   Incised and scraped decoration. Vamp,
quarters and latchet insert from side-latchet shoe
(late 14th-century; for reconstruction see Fig. 50).
Scale 1:3.

Fig. 121d has been decorated with a combination of engraving and of scraping back parts of the leather for contrast. Once more the effect is symmetrical, with three main areas of decoration based on a design of simple lanceolate leaves. The marking out of decorative areas in advance is clearly illustrated on this piece, for there has been a slight miscalculation as regards the size and placement of the upper left leaf. If the border was still to be done when the main decoration was engraved, it would have been possible to adjust the line of the border to fit the leaf-tip, rather than chop it off.

The fragment shown in Fig. 121a also has engraved and scraped foliate decoration, again based

on symmetrically-placed three-leaf designs which were easily adapted to suit the shapes and corners to be filled. The outline of the pattern, the internal details on the leaves and the margin around the outside have all been delineated with engraving, and the areas between have been lightly scraped away to create a contrasting background colour. The shoe in Fig. 121b has the same basic techniques and elements of design, but the leaves have been stylised and simplified so that they are almost geometrically abstract.

121   Engraved and scraped decoration. Vamps and
quarters from buckle- or latchet-fastened shoes (all
late 14th-century). Scale 1:3.

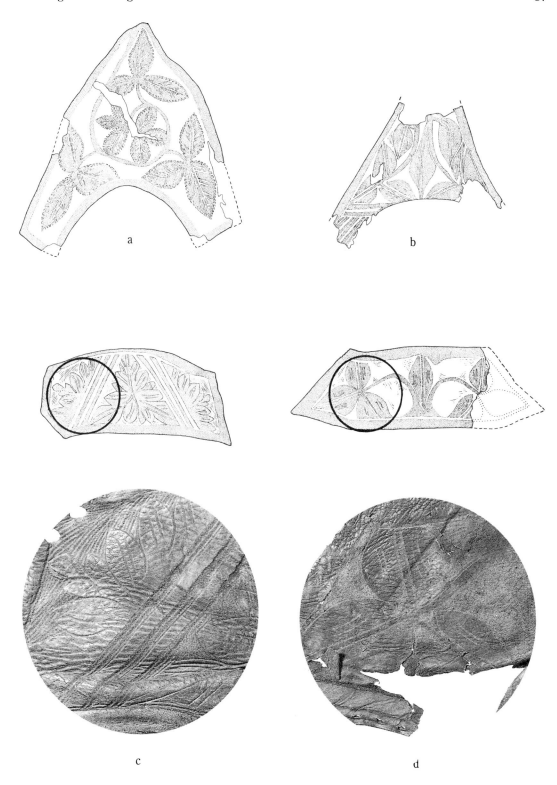

a

b

c

d

Toe stuffing (by Alan Eddy)

Most late 14th-century 'poulaines' were stuffed with moss so as to retain their shape (Fig. 122). In particular, the intention seems to have been to stiffen and bend the toe in such a way that it curled up from the ground and made walking a little easier. This is shown by the fact that the tips of some 'poulaines' are almost entirely unworn on the underside.

Moss from thirty-six different shoes was examined, and it is clear that one species, *Thuidium tamarascinum*, was by far the most popular, being the only or the major component in nearly two-thirds of the samples (23 examples). It is a profusely-branched moss with densely-arranged, very small, papillose leaves which make it springy and ideal for use as a filler (Fig. 122 detail); it would have, besides, significant absorbent properties – a potentially valuable attribute for the stuffing of a shoe. Only two other mosses, *Rhytidiadelphus triquetris* and *Eurhyncium striatum*, occur in any numbers (6 and 7 examples respectively). They have rather stiff, wiry stems and were probably chosen because they are conspicuous, can be gathered easily, adhering only loosely to the soil, and generally grow in considerable quantity.

All three mosses, together with six or seven others found in much smaller numbers, are characteristic of mixed woodland – probably oak or ash dominated – on neutral to basic soils. In medieval

122 Moss (*thuidium tamarascinum*) stuffing removed from 'poulaine' of late 14th-century side-latchet shoe (for line drawing see Figs. 49 & 104). Inset: highly-magnified view of modern *thuidium tamarascinum* (sample kindly provided by the British Museum (Natural History)).

times small areas of such woodland may have remained quite close to the City wall, but extensive areas would probably have been about ten miles distant, say, Enfield Chase to the north or the north Surrey woods to the south. One sample, however, *Pleurozium schreberi*, belongs in an entirely different environment. This is a calcifuge moss characteristic of heathland or acid woodland such as is still found today on Blackheath or Hampstead Heath.

The different species of moss do not seem to be associated with particular types or styles of shoe, but it seems significant that a small group of contemporary shoes from Gloucester, which was examined at the same time as the present samples, was stuffed with a higher proportion of riverine mosses. This may reinforce the obvious hypothesis that medieval shoes were generally made in the towns where they were sold and worn, rather than transported over long distances.

Repairs and Reuse

As has already been noted above, a large number of the shoes, especially the soles, have been subjected to some degree of repair and/or reuse (Tables 15–16). This is a topic upon which the surviving records of the London Cordwainers'

Company provide a fascinating commentary. The repairing of shoes gave rise to numerous disputes between cordwainers and cobblers, principally over the demarcation of their respective fields of business. It seems that the original trade of the cobbler was not simply that of repairing shoes – a worn shoe would normally be returned to the shoemaker ('cordwainer') for repair – but rather that of dealing in second-hand shoes, principally, one assumes, for the benefit of the poor. He would buy up old shoes, recondition them and then resell them. It was the process of reconditioning that caused conflict with the cordwainers – in particular, the extent to which *new* leather could be used. A ruling of 1409 prohibited cobblers from using new leather for soles or quarters, but permitted them to 'clout old boots and shoes with new leather upon the old soles, before or behind' (Mander 1931, 56); 'resoling' and any other repairs with new leather were to be done by cordwainers.

Resoling – presumably the replacement of a worn sole by an entirely new one – must have been time-consuming, since it will have involved the restitching of the entire lasting-margin, and it may be for this reason that many soles were made in two parts: the heel could be replaced, but not

---

Table 15. Numbers of shoes that have been repaired.

	Soles			Uppers		
	total	repairs	%	total	repairs	%
Seal House (early/mid 13th c.)	17	6	35.3	29	1	3.6
Swan Lane (late 13th c.)	15	8	53.3	44	4	9.1
'Baynards Castle' (mid 14th c.)	33	11	33.3	32	1	3.1
'Baynards Castle' (late 14th c.)	282	25	8.9	303	13	4.3
Swan Lane (early/mid 15th c.)	67	37	55.2	144	1	0.7
Trig Lane (early/mid 15th c.)	101	28	27.7	342	3	0.9

Table 16. Numbers of shoes that have been cut up for reuse of the leather.

	Soles			Uppers		
	total	reused	%	total	reused	%
Seal House (early/mid 13th c.)	17	—	—	29	6	20.7
Swan Lane (late 13th c.)	15	—	—	44	18	40.9
'Baynards Castle' (mid 14th c.)	33	4	12.1	32	15	46.9
'Baynards Castle' (late 14th c.)	282	21	7.5	303	76	25.1
Swan Lane (early/mid 15th c.)	67	—	—	144	13	9.0
Trig Lane (early/mid 15th c.)	101	3	3.0	342	42	12.3

the forepart, or *vice versa*. It is impossible to identify with certainty any shoes in the collection that
have been resoled in this way, although abnormal
clusters of stitches along the lasting-margins of
the upper indicate that some have been at least
partially remade.

Very much more common are separate repair-
soles of the type that should apparently be attributed only to cobblers. These 'clumps' are thick,
irregularly-shaped pieces of leather and were
attached with tunnel-stitching (Fig. 123). Normally, separate pieces were used for the heel and
forepart. The sole and its clump occasionally
survive together (Figs. 94, 98) but more often the
only evidence that a shoe has been 'clouted' is
provided by stitch-marks, either on the sole (Fig.
83) or low down on the upper (Figs. 84, 106). As
Table 15 shows, over half the shoes in some
groups have repair-soles, and it is tempting to

infer from this that they may have had two, if not
more, owners before they were finally discarded.
Equally striking is the very low proportion (less
than 10 per cent) in the late 14th-century 'Baynards Castle' group. Since, theoretically at least,
this should imply that the former owners of the
rubbish discarded in the inlet could afford new
rather than reconditioned shoes, and even
perhaps that they had them repaired by accredited
cordwainers, then again (see above, p. 29) we
might speculate that this deposit represents an
above-average stratum of society.

Comparatively few uppers in any of the groups
seem to have been repaired (Table 15). Occasionally, additional stitch impressions suggest that a
seam has been remade, but the most common
type of repair is a patch sewn in on the inside of the
shoe with binding-stitch (in the manner of a heel-
stiffener or lace-hole reinforcement) to cover a
worn area or hole. One of the clearest examples of
this is shown in Fig. 104: here, two successive
patches appear to have been added to strengthen
the side seam, perhaps after the shoe had split
apart. Repairs of this kind seem not to have been
common, however, probably because the soles
will have worn through long before the uppers,
rendering many shoes worthless after only a few
months' use.

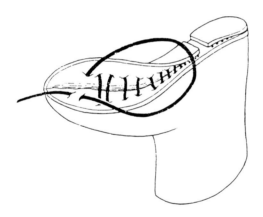

123 Method used to attach repair soles ('clumps').
These invariably came in two sections – heel and
forepart – and were sewn on with tunnel-stitches,
which were often widely-spaced and irregular. When
all the stitches had been made, the thread would have
been pulled tight and tied.

Pattens

Medieval shoes can rarely have been fully water-proof, and the flat heels must have made walking additionally unpleasant in mud or snow. Several types of overshoe were devised to raise the foot further above the ground, and in the 14th and 15th centuries these were variously known as pattens ('patyns'), clogs ('clogges') or galoshes ('galoches'). The original meanings of these terms are unclear. They do not necessarily correspond to those that have become customary since the 17th century, and for convenience 'patten' is used here as a general term to cover three similar, though plainly distinguishable, types of overshoe that are well-known finds on archaeological sites both in London and elsewhere (in Amsterdam, for example: Baart *et al.* 1977, 83–91, Figs. 16–18, 20–22). One type has a wooden 'platform' sole raised from the ground on 'stilts' or wedges (Figs. 125–7), another has a flat wooden sole, which was often hinged (Figs. 133, 135–6), and the third has a flat composite sole made from several layers of leather (Figs. 139–40).

In comparison with shoes, pattens seem never to have been common in London before the early 15th century (Table 21, p. 132). This, together with the fact that many are elaborately decorated, suggests that in the City, especially during the late 14th century, they were worn chiefly as a useful fashion accessory to protect the feet – and the shoes – of the well-to-do. The early 15th-century groups, on the other hand, which contain large numbers of all-leather composite-soled pattens and a higher proportion of flat, hinged pattens (Table 21), hint both at a change in fashion and that by this time pattens had come to be worn by the population in general. This impression is confirmed by the more frequent depiction of pattens in late medieval illustrations (see below, p. 119), some of which (for example, Bagley 1960, 142) make it clear that they might be worn no longer as true overshoes, but rather over the hose as a fashionable form of open sandal.

Wooden pattens, 12th–15th centuries
(Figs. 125, 132)

The earliest patten fragment in the collection is part of a plain toe strap from Seal House dating from the early 12th century, but the earliest complete patten, coincidentally from the same site, belongs to the early 13th century (Fig. 126). It is crudely but solidly constructed, carved from a single block of alder with a straight-sided sole and a wedge below the ball of the foot. The front has been sawn diagonally to suit a left foot, but this has been done so roughly that it seems more likely to be a modification carried out during use than an original feature. This is the only patten in the collection to have iron fittings – a reinforcement-

124 A patten-maker shaping a wooden sole with an adze. Four draw-knives, probably used for preliminary roughing-out, hang in a rack on the wall behind. (From the Mendel Housebook (Nuremberg), late 15th century).

125 Wooden pattens, 13th/14th-century, with soles raised on wedges above ground level. For line drawings see Figs. 126 & 127.

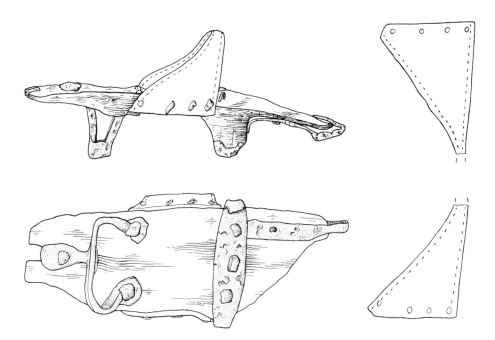

126 Wooden patten (early 13th-century). Clenched iron nails hold the iron stand at the back and the reinforcement strip covering the carved wedge beneath the ball of the foot. The leather toe strap is also nailed on, and rows of grain/flesh stitches suggest that it was originally bound with leather edging (cf. Fig. 127). The forepart has been roughly sawn to shape, and an iron strip has been nailed on and folded over. Scale 1:3.

piece at the toe, a protective strip beneath the wedge and a stand under the heel. The toe strap was held to the sides with iron nails and, although broken, seems originally to have been a single piece of leather.

By far the largest group of wooden pattens may be assigned to the second half of the 14th century, the product of excavations at 'Baynards Castle', Billingsgate and Trig Lane (Table 21). The soles are mostly in poor condition, but at least one resembled the earlier Seal House example, having a sole shaped from one block, with wedges to raise it high off the ground (Fig. 127). Yet it is much more carefully finished and, to judge from the presence of a third wedge beneath the toes, the sole may have extended into a long 'poulaine' to conform with the most fashionable shoes of the period. There was a single broad band over the

toes, made from two pieces of leather joined at the centre and decorated with stamped florets, but some pattens of this date were provided with toe bands that were adjustable (Figs. 128–131). This was normally done by passing a strap on one side through a slit in a strap on the other and pinning the two together with an iron nail. The example in Fig. 130 shows a variation whereby one strap was bifurcated and a pair of slits and nails was used.

With practice it would have been possible to walk quite normally in pattens such as those illustrated in Figs. 126–7 by rocking from one wedge to another, but many late 14th-century pattens had soles which rested flat on the ground (Figs. 128, 133–4). Some had long 'poulaines', and it was probably so that they could be worn more easily by those accustomed to ordinary shoes that they were made in two parts which were hinged together. This will have allowed the patten to flex with the tread of the foot. Normally the hinge was a double-thickness leather strip nailed into a rebate in the sole (Fig. 133); but one example (not illustrated), which is fragmentary and, unusually, of beech (*fagus* sp.) rather than alder or willow/poplar, may have had a complete leather sole nailed across the heel and forepart to act as a hinge and, at the same time, to make it more comfortable to wear.

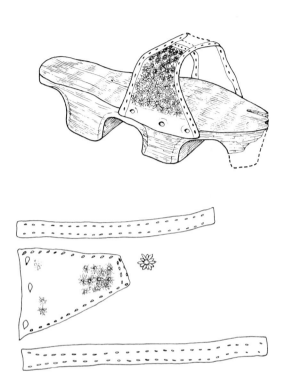

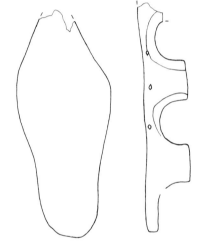

127

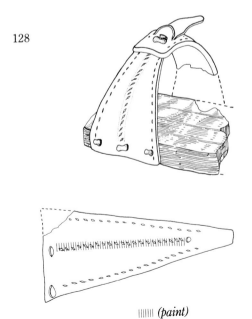

128

128 Patten fragment (mid/late 14th-century). The leather straps are double-thickness, and at least one of them was decorated with a red-painted stripe (marked with dotted lines); there was probably no binding at the edges, because the nails clearly pass over the stitch-holes (contrast Fig. 127). The fastening was effected simply with an iron nail. Scale 1:3.

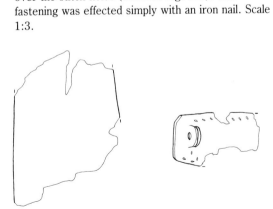

|||||| *(paint)*

127 (*left*) Wooden patten (mid/late 14th-century). Carved from a single block but now broken off at the toe. The leather toe strap is decorated with stamped florets (the enlarged detail shows the form of the stamp used) and was nailed in place; it was made from two symmetrical pieces joined at the centre (one piece missing) and its edges were strengthened with leather binding (surviving completely) folded double over them. Scale 1:3.

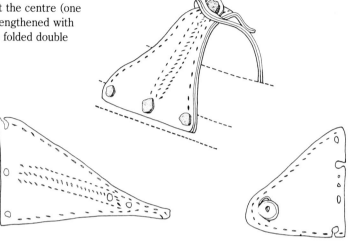

129 Patten straps (late 14th-century). Double-thickness leather. Scale 1:3.

130 Patten straps (late 14th-century). Single-thickness leather. Scale 1:3.

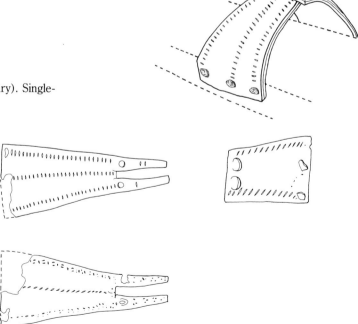

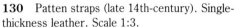

It was also in the late 14th century that heel straps were provided for the first time. The fragment shown in Fig. 134 was made from two layers of leather – one of which is now mostly lost – sewn together along the edges with a binding stitch and nailed to the sole at the sides and heel. To protect the leather from chafing under the nail heads was a thin leather strip which acted as a 'washer' and probably ran completely around the sole. The strap itself probably extended over the instep and was fastened with a buckle, as on a patten recently excavated on the City of London Boys' School site (in 1986, too late to be included in this volume).

Hinged wooden pattens with flat soles continued to be worn in the first half of the 15th century. The type raised on wedges is surprisingly absent from both Trig Lane and Swan Lane, though its continuing popularity is attested both by contemporary illustrations and surviving examples in the established collections of the Museum of London (see below, p. 119). Early 15th-century pattens had extremely waisted soles and rather blunt,

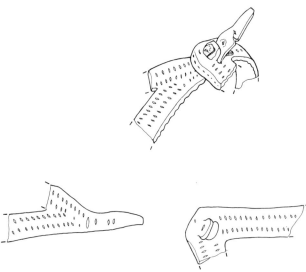

131 Patten straps (mid/late 14th-century). Scale 1:3.

132 Composite leather-soled patten and hinged wooden pattens (late 14th/early 15th-century). For line drawings see Figs. 133, 136 & 140.

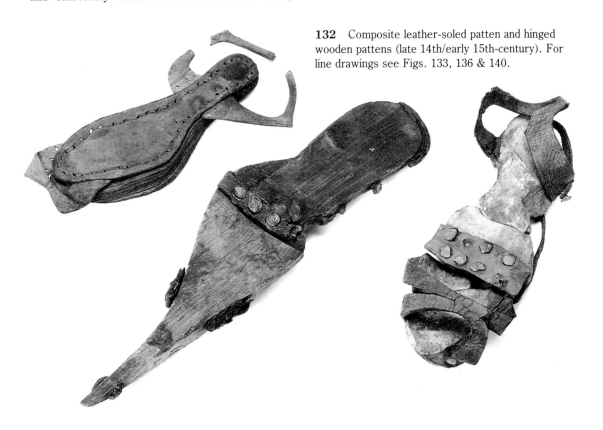

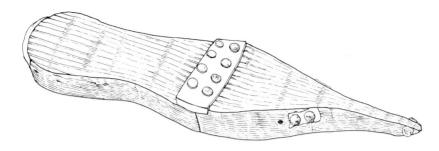

133 Wooden patten sole (late 14th-century). The two parts probably belong together, although one has been securely identified as alder (*alnus* sp.) and the other as possibly willow or poplar (*salicaceae*). The single-thickness leather hinge is nailed into a rebate, and nails at the toe and at the tip of the 'poulaine' show the position of the straps and leather edging-strip (part of which survives at the heel; cf. Fig. 134). Scale 1:3.

134 Wooden patten (late 14th-century). The leather back-strap was originally double-thickness throughout, and the scalloped edge suggests that the layers were held together with binding-stitch. Scale 1:3.

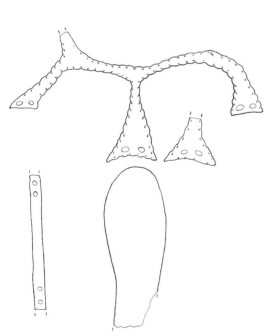

oval-shaped toes, to match the shoe fashions of the time, and were provided with straps at both the heel and the toe (Figs. 135–6). In comparison with the broad bands common in the 14th century and earlier, these straps were narrow and insubstantial, similar to those used with the contemporary leather-soled pattens (see below), and the toe strap was set much further forward. This was probably because of the flexible sole, which will have responded more precisely to the movements of the foot and will have caused less stress over the instep. The straps themselves were attached with nails and, as before, a strip running along the edge of the sole behind the nail heads protected them from chafing and provided a more finished appearance.

The woods used in the soles have been identified by Rowena Gale, whose conclusions are summarised in Table 17. This shows that, apart from the beech fragment mentioned above, just two groups are definitely present – alder (*alnus* sp.) and woods of the family *Salicaceae*. The latter includes both willow (*salix* sp.) and poplar (*populus*

Table 17. The wood used for patten soles.

| | *Alnus* sp. | | *Salicaceae* | | *Fagus* sp. | Unidenti- | Total |
	certain	possible	certain	possible	possible	fiable	
13th–early 14th c.	1	1	—	—	—	—	2
Late 14th c.	2	—	2	2	1	1	8
Early 15th c.	3	2	3	1	—	1	10
Total	6	3	5	3	1	2	20

135 Wooden patten (early/mid 15th-century). The leather hinge is nailed into a rebate, and nails hold the thick, single-layer back-strap. Scale 1:3.

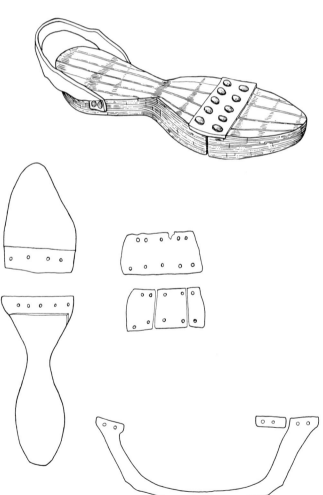

sp.), but the genera cannot be distinguished anatomically. Alder is soft and light, with a smooth grain that is easily worked. Resilient and extremely durable when wet, it has been the favourite material for clog-making in England right up to the present day (Vigeon 1977, 2). In modern times it has been normal practice to cut out the soles roughly when the wood is still green, to leave them to dry out, and then to complete the final shaping after any initial shrinkage has occurred. A similar method was probably used in the medieval period also, as indeed might be inferred from the illustration in the Mendel Housebook (Fig. 124) which shows drawknives hanging on the wall – presumably to be used for preliminary roughing-out – and a small adze being used for trimming.

Among the willows and poplars several species might be suitable for patten-making. *Salix alba* and *salix fragilis* are lightweight and tough, with a resistance to splintering. Although not generally very durable, they will last almost indefinitely if kept constantly wet and for this reason were used more recently to make paddles for waterwheels and steamers. *Populus nigra*, now fairly rare but

136 Wooden patten (early/mid 15th-century), complete. The straps are of single-thickness, the hinge of double-thickness, cattle-hide. Scale 1:3.

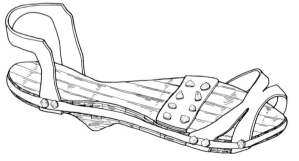

used extensively by medieval craftsmen, is hard and easily worked, but perishable. Yet, rather than any of these, it is tempting to suppose that the present items are of aspen, *populus tremula*. In modern France it has been used for sabots, but in medieval England it was specifically prohibited as a material for patten-making by a well-known law of 1416 (*4 Hen v c.3*). The purpose of this statute seems to have been to preserve the wood for making arrows and to keep the price of arrows down, since half the hundred-shilling fine levied on those who failed to observe it was to be paid to the Fletchers. Nearly fifty years later, in 1464–5, after strenuous representations by the patten-makers, who claimed that 'Asp timber be the best and lightest Timber, thereof to make Pattens and Clogs', it was enacted that pattens could

henceforth be made of 'such Timber of Asp, that is not apt, sufficient, nor convenient to be made into (arrowshafts)' (*4 Edw iv c.9*).

The leather straps were made from stout cattle-hide and on many late 14th-century pattens were of double thickness (Figs. 128–9). The two pieces were stitched together along the sides, with the flesh faces together and, sometimes, a thin leather edging to give a less ragged appearance. In the 12th and 13th centuries, and again in the early 15th, the straps were plain, but the broad bands of the late 14th century provided an ideal opportunity for embellishment. Nearly all carry some decoration, however slight. One (Fig. 128) has a narrow vertical stripe, once painted in brilliant red. The pigment used was vermillion (identified by S. Duncan, British Museum), which was well known to medieval artists and could either be made artificially or could be obtained from cinnabar, the principal ore of the metal mercury. Others have stamped ornament, two of them, from Billingsgate (Fig. 127) and 'Baynards Castle' (not illustrated),

137 Leather patten-straps (late 14th-century). *a*: stamped decoration (the enlarged detail shows the form of the stamp used), *b–f*: stitched decoration (for the possible form of the stitch, see Fig. 138). Scale 1:3.

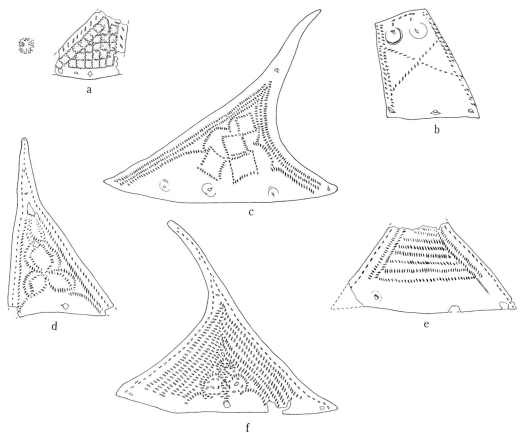

an identical all-over floral pattern. The motif itself, consisting of four larger petals between pairs of smaller petals, was apparently made with a single punch stamped at random, for except at the edges the impressions are not in neat rows but sometimes overlap. The third stamped fragment (Fig. 137a) has a geometric design, evidently made up of wavy-edged squares, but it is too worn and distorted to allow the exact form of the punch to be reconstructed.

The most common means of decoration was by stitching, but since few of the threads have survived it is not certain how the seams would have looked originally. It is possible that a simple running-stitch was used but more probable that it was a type of back-stitching (Fig. 138), for this would have produced a continuous rather than an intermittent line. The stitch-holes are rarely cir-

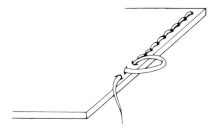

138   Back-stitching, the stitch probably used on at least some patten-straps. Only one thread is needed. The perforations, as on many straps (cf. Fig. 137), are oblique and rectangular rather than circular, so that the thread is pulled from the top corner of one to the bottom corner of the next.

cular; normally they are slanting, rectangular slits, so that the thread would not have lain in a straight line but would have been pulled tight at an angle from the top corner of one to the bottom corner of the next – a form of semi-ornamental seam commonly used today by harness-makers and saddlers (Salamon 1986, 273–4 and Fig. 9.64). Various simple patterns were devised to fit into the awkward shape of the straps: vertical or horizontal lines (Figs. 128–30), either singly or in rows and perhaps once highlighted by threads of contrasting colours, crosses (Fig. 137b) and lozenges or leaves within arcaded niches (Figs. 137c–d). More complicated series of stitch-holes (Figs. 137e–f) may be the remnant of very elaborate designs, now incapable of reconstruction.

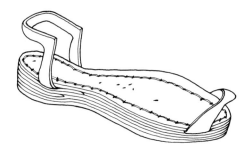

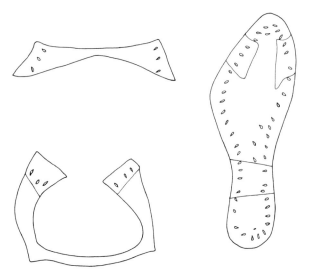

139   Leather patten (late 13th-century). The sole has six main layers with an additional segment, making a seventh, at the heel. Deep impressions mark the original position of the thread and show how tightly it was pulled. Scale 1:3.

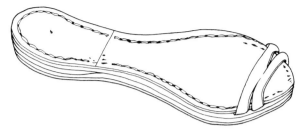

140 Leather patten (early 15th-century). Four-layer sole (five layers at the heel). The top layer was made from two parts butt-stitched together. Scale 1:3.

Leather pattens, 14th–15th centuries
(Figs. 139–40)

In later medieval times a new form of patten with a composite leather sole and narrow heel and toe straps became fashionable. As Table 21 shows, these were probably introduced in the late 13th or early 14th century but were extremely rare before the early 15th; thereafter they seem to have been quite common, although it should be remembered that the large number of fragments, mainly from the composite soles, probably represents no more than a fifth as many complete pattens. The soles themselves were made from layers of thick cattle hide, generally between 5 and 7 but sometimes as many as 10, and it is likely that they were sewn together with a pair of threads (Fig. 141), which have left deep impressions in the upper and lower surfaces of the top and bottom layers respectively (Figs. 139–40). An additional layer was often added at the heel only, so as to raise it higher off the ground. The straps were made from single pieces of plain leather, sometimes bifurcated at the toe (Fig. 140), and were sandwiched between the top layer and the layer immediately beneath it.

Pattens of this type were generally quite narrow, no broader than the average shoe, with a pronounced 'waist' and a slightly pointed toe. This, together with the fact that there can have been very little room under the toe straps, would be consistent with the suggestion made earlier that they should perhaps be regarded as sandals rather than overshoes. The weakest element in their construction was the stitching, which was exposed to damp on the underside of the sole and must often have perished. Many pattens have additional rows, or part rows, of stitch holes to show that they were restitched, sometimes on several occasions. One (Fig. 142), which is exceptionally heavily worn at the heel, seems to have had an undersole nailed on as a final repair.

142 Leather patten (early/mid 15th-century). Four layers survive. The parallel seams around the edges show that the sole was restitched on at least one occasion. A whole additional layer was nailed onto the underside as a final repair. Scale 1:3.

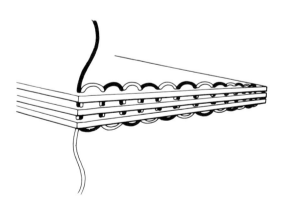

141 Interlocking running-stitch, using two threads, the type of stitch that would have been used in the manufacture of multi-layered patten-soles (cf. Figs. 139–40).

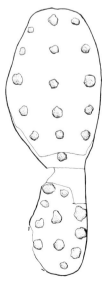

Sizes and wear patterns: social inferences

Sizes

Footwear assemblages as large as those from London can provide useful statistical information about the sizes of medieval shoes and pattens. This data, in turn, can make it possible to draw some conclusions about the use of footwear in the City and, to some extent, about the physical characteristics of the population. The present study is, regrettably, confined to the conserved registered shoes. The unconserved bulk fragments would have formed a much larger sample – at least of complete soles – but many were found to be too distorted for accurate measurement and the remainder seemed to produce aberrant results, apparently because they had shrunk at different rates.

Table 19, which covers the four largest groups of registered footwear, was prepared by measuring the maximum overall length of the shoe soles in each group and then converting the measurements to give their size according to the modern English Shoe-Size Scales (Table 18). In the case of shoes with 'poulaines', the 'poulaine' itself was discounted and the measurement taken to a point on or just beyond the estimated extremity of the big toe (see above, pp. 29–31 and Table 8). Modern shoe sizes represent the *inside* measurement of the shoe within the upper, rather than the length of the sole; but since turn-shoe uppers tended to oversail their soles when in use, especially at the heel, measurement of the sole is likely to produce an under- rather than an overestimate of the equivalent size.

The purpose of the conversion to modern sizes is partly to make the measurements more readily intelligible and partly to facilitate comparison with other statistical data. Medieval shoemakers presumably made shoes to measure (bespoke) or, if for general stock, with just sufficient variations in size to enable the average customer to select a suitable pair by trial and error. There is no reason to suppose that they observed specific size standards, and the fragmentary records of the London Cordwainers' Company make no mention of such. Nor, to judge

from measurements taken across the forepart, waist and heel of shoes from Swan Lane and Trig Lane, does it seem that shoes were made in a range of width fittings: the width of the shoe normally varied in direct proportion to its length, although as observed with the shoes from Kings Lynn (Clarke & Carter 1977, 355), it appears that between the 12th and the 15th centuries the waist became progressively narrower.

Simple measurements are unfortunately only a rough approximation to the original size of an excavated shoe. Not only may the leather have been distorted by the long period of burial, but it may also have shrunk since recovery, both during and after the processes of conservation. Since little is so far known about the potential changes in medieval leather *after* laboratory treatment, no adjustment has been made for this, but shrinkage *during* treatment has been quantified and can, to some extent, be predicted: freeze-dried leather

Table 18. Shoe sizes according to the English and Continental Shoe-Size Scales

Length (mm)	Length (inches)	English sizes	Continental sizes
110	4⅓	child's 1	16½
119	4⅔	child's 2	18
128	5	child's 3	19
136	5⅓	child's 4	20½
144	5⅔	child's 5	22
153	6	child's 6	23
161	6⅓	child's 7	24
170	6⅔	child's 8	26
178	7	child's 9	27
187	7⅓	child's 10	28
195	7⅔	child's 11	29
204	8	child's 12	30½
212	8⅓	child's 13	31½
221	8⅔	adult 1	33
229	9	adult 2	34
238	9⅓	adult 3	35½
246	9⅔	adult 4	37
254	10	adult 5	38
263	10⅓	adult 6	39½
271	10⅔	adult 7	41
280	11	adult 8	42

seems to shrink by no more than *c*.5 per cent, whereas solvent-drying – the older method – can cause a reduction of up to *c*.10 per cent (pp. 138–9 and Table 22). To produce Table 19, therefore, the 'raw' measurements from the soles themselves were increased by one or other of these percentages, in accordance with the conservation method used for each batch (see Table 21).

It remains quite impossible, however, to account for any shrinkage which may have occurred *before* conservation, when the object was still buried. John Thornton began an experiment in 1959, in which he buried in wet soil a series of oak-tanned leather strips that could be removed for measurement at intervals of 1, 2, 4, 8, 16, 32, 64 and 128 years (see Rhodes 1980, 101–2). This seems to have suggested that leather shrinks very rapidly at first but that the rate decreases thereafter (the strips shrank by *c*.7 per cent after 4 years, by 9¼ per cent after 8 years and by 9½ per cent after 16 years), perhaps until an overall reduction of *c*.10 per cent is reached. More recently, however, Carol van Driel-Murray has argued that Roman shoes, at least, have shrunk much less during burial than after recovery (*Archaeological Leather Group Newsletter*, **2**, Winter 1986/7), a hypothesis that seems to be receiving general acceptance and that would make far better sense of the present collection. If an *additional* factor of 10 per cent were applied to the figures already adjusted for post-excavation shrinkage, it would lead to the unexpected conclusion that medieval shoes were little different in size from their modern counterparts.

Yet, however much the shoes may have shrunk in *absolute* terms, it seems that their *relative* sizes have been preserved intact. It can hardly be coincidental that the three largest groups shown in Table 19 (from 'Baynards Castle', Swan Lane and Trig Lane) share a distribution of sizes that is so similar, both overall and in detail. All three graphs have two peaks – the higher at adult sizes 4–5, the lower at adult sizes 1–3 or 2–3 – and it is difficult to avoid the inference that these correspond to the most popular sizes of adult men's and women's shoes. In modern Britain nine-tenths of the adult male population wears shoes ranging from sizes 6 to 11, and nine-tenths of the adult female population shoes ranging from 4 to 8 (Clarks Ltd. 1972, Figs. 12–13). Figures from modern France are broadly comparable: *c*.60 per cent of adult males

are fitted with sizes 6–9 and *c*.60 per cent of adult females with sizes 4–7 (*Technicuir* (1980–1), Tableaux 4–5; information from Claire Symonds). All these statistics, both medieval and modern, would thus be consistent in indicating a difference of 2 or 3 sizes between the male and female peaks.

If this is so, it may be possible to proceed further and to use historical data to calibrate medieval shoe measurements, as a check on the shrinkage rates estimated by empirical means. Surveys conducted by Clarks Ltd. over the past hundred years indicate that the average foot is growing at the rate of one size every 20 years or so (information from Neil MacDonald). In the late 19th and early 20th centuries sizes 2–7 were most popular among men, and sizes 1–4 among women. The width of the foot has increased in proportion, so that whereas sizes D–F were most common in 1972, sizes C–E were most common in 1953 and sizes B–D in 1929 (Clarks Ltd. 1972, Table D, with additions). These figures from late Victorian England correspond broadly to those from medieval London as stated in Table 19, and, representing as they do a population unaffected by modern dietary developments, may be as accurate an estimate as any of the stature of the medieval population and of the original size of the shoes illustrated in this volume. And, as an additional scrap of corroborative evidence, it is impossible to overlook the information from the late 1st/early 3rd-century Roman forts and civilian settlements at Saalburg, Zugmantel and Kleiner Feldburg (Table 19; after Groenman-van Waateringe 1974, Fig. 11; figures converted to modern sizes by M. Rhodes and adjusted by 10 per cent for presumed solvent-drying), where a very similar range of sizes has again been recorded.

Although it may be possible to identify the *general* range of sizes befitting medieval men and women, the overlap between them and with the children's range (see below) makes it much more difficult to determine whether an *individual* shoe was worn by a man or a woman. This in turn frustrates the attempt to distinguish specifically male from female fashions. The present finds hint that in the 13th century the side-laced shoe was essentially a man's shoe, whereas the low draw-string ankle-shoe was more often worn by women and children (see above, p. 17), but the groups are too small to prove this conclusively. Indeed the only styles which can reasonably be identified as

Table 19   The range of shoe sizes from Seal House (early/mid 13th-century), 'Baynards Castle' (late 14th-century), Swan Lane (early 15th-century), Trig Lane (early/mid 15th-century) and several Continental Roman sites (see text; after Groenman-van Waateringe 1974, Fig. 11). The histogram represents the percentage of shoes of each size, with the **actual** numbers of shoes printed within or just above each bar.

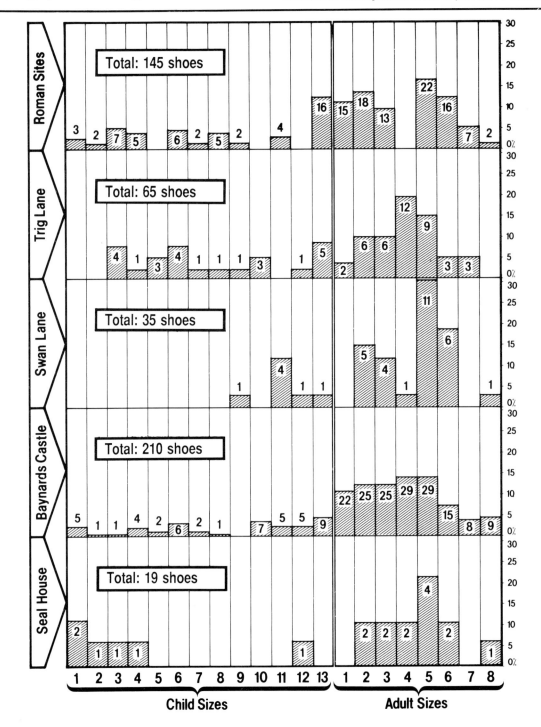

Child Sizes   Adult Sizes

men's wear are the late 14th-century buckled and side-latchet shoes (see above, pp. 32–3 and Table 9). These, it should be noted, generally have the longest 'poulaines' and are the most likely to be decorated. Normally, men and women appear to have worn the *same* styles – at least to judge by the evidence from Trig Lane (early/mid 15th century), where the adult size distribution of 20 side-laced boots or ankle-shoes shows the standard male and female peaks, and mirrors the distribution of this and other groups as a whole (Table 12). Social factors could be held at least partially responsible for this: it may be that the London finds are essentially utilitarian working-wear, and that it is only among the shoes of the higher grades of society – of which the 'Baynards Castle' group may be the sole representative – that distinctively male and female fashions can be recognised.

Children's shoes are a significant component of all the main assemblages except, surprisingly, that from Swan Lane. The smallest are very tiny indeed, corresponding to the modern children's sizes 1–3 (Table 19). The smallest shoes commonly made today are of children's size 5 and fit children aged about 12 months (Clarks Ltd. 1972, Fig. 14). This discrepancy of about 4 sizes between the medieval and modern statistics matches precisely that noted for the adult sizes, and so it seems reasonable to conclude that the smallest medieval shoes were similarly worn by infants not much more than a year old. The remaining children's shoes are evenly distributed through all the children's sizes and will probably have overlapped with the smallest adult sizes at a point when, to judge by modern statistics, the children were aged about eleven or twelve.* This accounts for the sharp rise in the number of shoes of adult sizes 1 or larger, but there are too many variables – the likelihood of shoes being handed down within the family, for example, or the antici-pated high rate of mortality among infants – for it to be possible to deduce the proportion of all medieval children that wore shoes or the proportion that did not wear shoes until they were five or even ten.

---

* Clarks Ltd. 1972, Fig. 14 (adult sizes 4 and 5 worn by eleven-year-old girls and boys respectively); *Technicuir* (1980–1), Tableaux 4–5 (similar sizes, but worn by girls and boys aged twelve or thirteen).

But despite the problems of interpretation there can be no doubt that many medieval children *did* wear shoes. Of the 210 shoes from 'Baynards Castle' 19 per cent are in children's sizes, as are 29 per cent of the 65 from Trig Lane (Table 19). This rise of 10 per cent from the late 14th to the early/mid 15th centuries may itself, if corrobor-ated by future findings, prove to be significant, for it was at this time that shoe styles particularly suitable for children were being developed. In the late 14th century nearly all children's shoes were front-laced (Table 9), though some were low-cut and pointed in imitation of the contemporary adult styles. Others, however, were low ankle-shoes, correspondingly more 'sensible' in style, and it was these which were to become common as children's shoes – though now fastened with a buckle – in the early 15th century. Nearly all range between children's sizes 3 and 9 (Table 12) and so would probably have been worn by children aged between about 2 and 6 years.

Pattens, whether of wood or leather, seem never to have been worn by the youngest infants. Even so, the smallest of the composite-soled pattens measures just 158 mm (roughly equiva-lent to the modern children's size 8) and the example illustrated in Fig. 139 is no more than 180 mm long (children's size 11). Pattens such as these seem too small to have been worn by adults or adolescents, but they might have been suitable for older children aged between six or seven and about eleven years. Otherwise, as Table 20 shows, there appears to have been an extensive range of sizes, very similar in overall distribution to that of ordinary shoes. Small peaks can be seen near the modern adult sizes 3 and 4–5 (*cf.* Fig. 140, *c.*244 mm long, modern adult size 5), which may have been the sizes most often selected by adult men and women, but the sample (just 24 registered pattens with complete soles) is too small to provide more detailed statistical information.

Wear patterns and deformities of the feet

The possibility of learning about the health of London's medieval population from the wear pat-terns on their shoes was first identified by Swallow (1975), who drew examples mainly from the late 14th-century 'Baynards Castle' assem-blage. The following paragraphs draw heavily upon his main arguments and suggestions. Few of

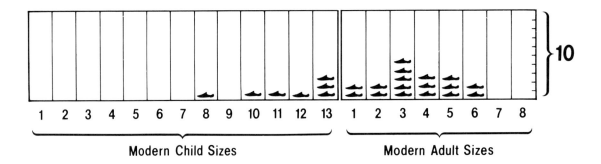

Modern Child Sizes   Modern Adult Sizes

the shoes found subsequently have been suffi-ciently well preserved to provide detailed evi-dence, at least of pathological conditions; but in any case it may be that standards of foot health were particularly poor in the late 14th century owing to the tight, narrow shoe fashions which were worn not only by adults but by young child-ren. Modern research suggests that many of the disorders which become noticeable only in old or middle age can be attributed to the wearing of incorrectly-fitting shoes when young. A child's foot is not fully formed before the age of about eight years, and even a soft shoe can deform it without causing obvious discomfort (Clarks Ltd. 1972, 7–11).

The feet are complex levers, made up of many small moving parts which are subjected to heavy loads. For this reason, minor variations in gait are

common, as are malformations of the feet them-selves, either congenital or the result of trauma. In normal walking the first point to touch the ground is the back of the heel on the outer (lateral) side, for the structure of the ankle and leg joints is such as to cause the foot to point outwards, at an angle of about 5 degrees to the direction of walk-ing, at the beginning of each step (Fig. 143). From there the foot rolls inwards slightly to transfer the weight squarely across the metatarsal heads, the 'ball' of the foot; and, finally, contraction of muscles in the calf and in the foot itself propels the body forward, flexing the metatarso-phalangeal joints at the base of the toes and pressing the tips of the toes onto the ground. This explains the wear patterns visible on many soles (Fig. 144) and, because the heel hits the ground at an angle, preventing it from sitting squarely in the shoe, it

143 Typical movement of a shoe in normal walking.

144 Wear and distortion caused by normal walking (cf. Fig. 143). Wear can be seen at the heel on the outer (lateral) side, across the full width of the tread and at the tip of the toe; the upper has been pushed inwards at the heel. Late 14th-century.

also explains why the quarters often bulge out slightly on the inner (medial) side (Fig. 144).

Conversely, when the sole is most heavily worn on the inner side of the heel, it indicates that the owner's feet pointed inwards, rather than outwards, as he walked – the condition popularly known as 'pigeon-toed'. A particularly clear example of this is a shoe worn by a very small child (Fig. 145; for reconstruction, see above, Fig. 47). The quarters and the sole are both severely damaged and, because the shoe was distorted inwards even more than usual, it seems that the quarters began to split, were cut and restitched together. A more serious abnormality is signified by soles whose tread, under the metatarsal heads, is particularly heavily worn and whose heel is relatively untouched. This pattern suggests that the wearer shuffled along or, in extreme cases, walked entirely on his toes. Such a manner of walking is most often caused by weakness of the Achilles tendon, the ankle or the calf muscles, which restricts the movement of the foot and prevents it rocking easily from heel to toe. The result is that the foot is almost flat when it strikes the ground. The condition is quite common today, but the use of stacked heels on nearly all walking shoes makes it less noticeable.

145 Wear and distortion caused by 'pigeon-toed' walking. The greatest wear is on the inner (medial) side of the heel, and the upper has been forced inwards to the extent that it has split and been restitched on the outer side. Late 14th-century.

146 *Hallux valgus* ('bunion'). The severe patch of wear on this narrow pointed shoe is at just the point where the metatarso-phalangeal joint may be expected to swell and bulge outwards if the wearer suffers from this condition. The great toe inevitably becomes twisted in the direction of the other toes. Late 14th-century.

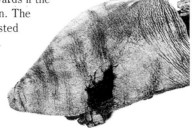

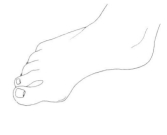

147 *Hallux rigidus*. Absence of wear on the tread, but a hole in a position to correspond with the tip of the great toe, suggests that the metatarso-phalangeal joint has been immobilised and that during walking the individual's weight has mostly been carried on the toe itself rather than on the ball of the foot. The cut-out in the upper was probably made to accommodate a swelling above the arthritic joint. Late 14th-century.

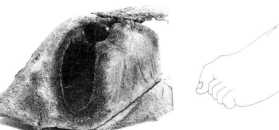

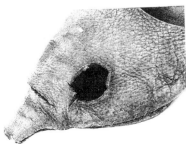

148 'Hammer toe'. Excessive wear on the tread suggests that the toes have become permanently flexed, probably because the individual has consistently worn shoes that are too narrow and tight. The cut-out in the upper was no doubt an attempt to relieve pressure on swellings above the damaged joints. Late 14th-century.

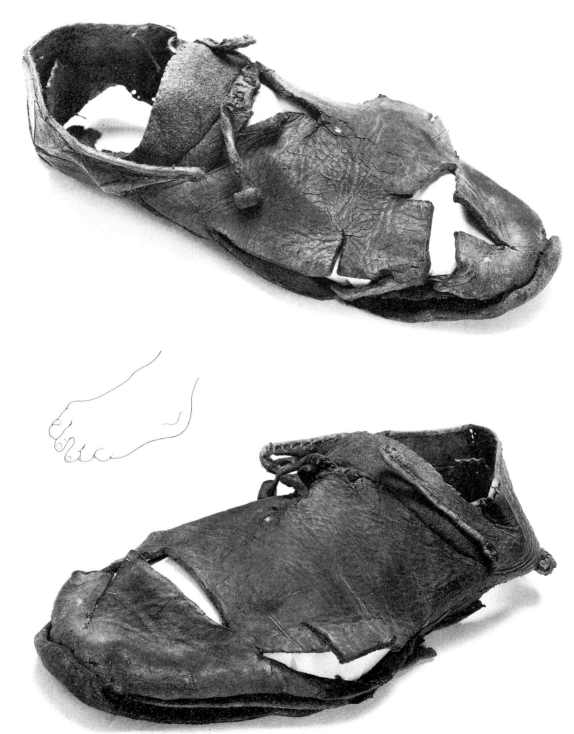

A feature of many shoes in the present collection is a slit in the vamp throat (Figs. 26, 50). In most cases this was probably made by wearers whose feet were abnormally arched and whose insteps would have rubbed uncomfortably, especially if the shoe was too small or too tightly cut. Other deliberate slits in the vamp and abnormal patches of wear on the upper or soles may signify deformities of the toes. One of the most common is the bunion (*hallux valgus*). This condition of the great toe (*hallux*) occurs when the metatarsal is displaced medially, causing the metatarso-phalangeal joint to bulge outwards and the great toe itself to turn inwards towards the other toes, sometimes even overlapping them (Fig. 146). The joint becomes enlarged and inflamed, so that a swelling, the 'bunion', develops on the side of the foot and rubs unpleasantly against the inside of the shoe. It is often thought that certain individuals have a natural propensity to the condition, perhaps only because their feet are disproportionately long, but it can be exacerbated by narrow, pointed or badly-fitting footwear. In medieval times there would have been no obvious remedy except to apply pads or to cut holes in the side of the shoe to relieve pressure, and it may be that slits low down on the inner side of uppers such as that illustrated (*cf.* Fig. 149) were made precisely for this purpose.

A rather different malformation of the great toe occurs when the metatarso-phalangeal joint becomes immobilised, usually through a form of osteoarthritis (*hallux rigidus*). This may either

149 *Hallux valgus*, combined with 'hammer toe'. Slits on the inner, outer and upper surfaces of the shoe indicate that a particularly severe bunion not only forced the lesser toes to retract and flex, but also displaced them sideways. Mid 14th-century.

occur naturally with age or be the result of trauma – repeated stubbing of the toe, for example. As the joint stiffens it prevents the toe from flexing fully, so that in walking much of the load is transferred from the metatarsal head at the 'ball' of the foot to the tip of the toe, flexing the interphalangeal joint in compensation (Fig. 147). The arthritic joint itself may become enlarged and a swelling may develop above it. Several shoes in the collection may have been worn by persons who suffered from this condition, because they have a small patch of excessive wear on the inner side of the sole in a position to correspond with the tip of the great toe (Fig. 147). On the illustrated examples there is also a cut-out in the vamp, which may have been made to relieve pressure on the swollen joint above.

The final condition to be described here, 'hammer toe', affects the lesser toes, especially the second, and occurs when the joints become rigid in such a way that the phalanges are permanently flexed in a clawed position (Fig. 148). This is often caused by narrow or pointed footwear which provides insufficient room for the toes and forces them to bend and turn inwards, but it may also accompany the common bunion: as the great toe becomes angled inwards it can drive its way in front of the second toe, making it flex and retract. One of the most obvious results of the disorder is a painful corn over the raised interphalangeal joint, which, without surgery, can be alleviated only by padding or by cutting out a section of the shoe upper. Several vamps in the collection have slits that may have been made for this reason, but the illustrated example seems to represent a particularly severe case, where a bunion has not only bent the toes upwards but has pushed them outwards: as a result, large cruciform slashes have been made in the top surface of the vamp and on both sides (Fig. 149).

Shoes in art and literature

The purpose of this final chapter is to bring together some of the divergent sources of information about medieval footwear and to compare the picture that they offer with that provided by the archaeological material in the present collection. It is also hoped briefly to compare the trends in shoe fashions evident in this country with contemporary trends on the Continent, by drawing both on the archaeological finds and on illustrative evidence. It is not possible to state conclusively that the manuscript evidence indicates one thing or another; only to convey impressions of what has been depicted. The quality of execution varies tremendously, as do the conventions used. The problem with assessing the evidence of footwear presented on tomb effigies or monumental brasses is that presumably one would choose to be shown in clothes approximating to, and in some cases surpassing, one's best. And it is worth noting that some brasses were of Flemish origin and imported, so that they may not represent strictly English fashions.

It seems unlikely that even the poorest people went barefoot, although they may have continued to wear their shoes when the stitching had gone and the soles were worn through (Fig. 150). People occasionally might go barefoot on pilgrimage as a form of penance, but with the exception of specifically biblical scenes, people depicted in medieval manuscripts are always shod. The 13th-century French poet Guillaume de Lorris, whose work was translated by Chaucer, made the following observation about the pride that even the lowliest members of society took in their appearance:

> *Of shoon and botes, newe and faire,*
> *Loke at the leest thou have a paire;*
> *And that they sitte so fetisly,*
> *That these rude may uttirly*
> *Merveyle, sith that they sitte so pleyn,*
> *How they come on or of ageyn.*
>
> (*The Romaunt of the Rose*, ed. Skeat 1912, 2265–70)

Chaucer himself uses a widower without shoes as

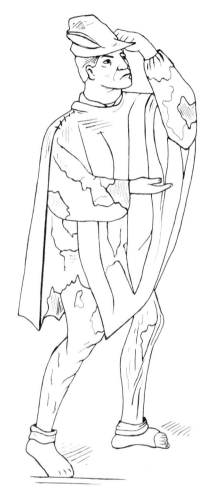

150   Beggar with tattered shoes and hose.

an example of extreme poverty in the Prologue to *The Canterbury Tales*:

> *For thogh a widwe hadde noght a sho,*
> *So plesaunt was his 'In principio',*
> *Yet wolde he have a ferthing, er he wente.*
> (ed. Skeat 1912, 253–5).

The *Treatise of Walter de Biblesworth* written in the early 14th century exhorts young boys to:

112

Put on your clothes dear children
Draw on your braies, shoes, gloves . . .
(quoted in Cunnington & Buck 1965, 14)

Thus, the first inference is that everyone wore shoes of some kind for some period of their lives. What type of shoes exactly remains to be seen.

Pictorial and literary parallels

Most of the 12th-century manuscripts in England which contain evidence of contemporary shoe fashions show figures wearing shoes cut high at the ankle, pointed but essentially shaped to the foot. Shoes with outwardly-curving points of exaggerated length, such as the two from London (Figs. 5–6), can be seen on several manuscripts decorated at the abbey of Citeaux in Burgundy in the early 12th century (Harris 1987), and are described in contemporary writings. William of Malmesbury (lib. iv; ed. Stubbs 1889, 369) claimed that they were introduced in the reign of Rufus, whilst Orderic Vitalis called them 'scorpions' tails' and contemptuously traced their origin to Count Fulk of Anjou, who had them made to disguise his deformed feet and bunions! Later, he says, one of Rufus's courtiers stuffed the toes of his shoes and bent them into the shape of a ram's horn (*Eccl. Hist.* lib. viii; Chibnall 1973, vol. iv, 136–9).

Illustrations sometimes show loose, low boots, high at the back of the ankle with diagonal lines that indicate the leather sagging about the foot. These may represent boots of soft leather, or they may be intended as buskins – low stockings of linen or silk, tied at the knee with a ribbon. It is most likely that buskins are indicated on the brasses and illustrations featuring members of ecclesiastical orders. Several such buskins do survive, including those of Archbishop Hubert Walter of Canterbury (d. 1205). These are of silk compound twill, with foliate crosses, eagles and stars embroidered in silver-gilt thread, and with tablet-woven ribbons at the top for fastening (King in Zarnecki *et al.* 1984, 358, No. 493a).

The most common form of decoration is the vamp stripe, sometimes on the feet of all the figures in a picture, but more usually on the shoes of a saint or king, presumably as an indication of status. The Virgin Mary also wears shoes with this decoration, from which we may infer that this was appropriate for women of high standing (Fig.

151 Shoes with a vamp stripe, as worn by the Virgin Mary.

151). Other decoration also occurs, such as overall dots. A mid 12th-century painting of John the Baptist in the chapel of St. Gabriel at Canterbury Cathedral shows all the attendant figures wearing shoes cut high at the ankle with a row of contrasting dots along the centre of the vamp, around the throat and as clusters of three on the quarters (Tristram 1944, Pl. 14). It is worth noting that by the early 13th century, vamp stripes have virtually disappeared on the shoes in the collection (see above, p. 12), whereas they continued to be an occasional feature on ecclesiastical brasses until the late 14th century. Fig. 152 shows the shoes of Robert de Waldeby, Archbishop of York (d. 1397), from his brass in Westminster Abbey: here, a wide stripe is indicated down the centre of the vamp.

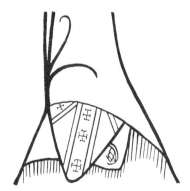

152 Detail from the brass of Robert de Waldeby, Archbishop of York (d.1397), in Westminster Abbey, showing a shoe or buskin with vamp stripe.

Very occasionally during the late 12th century, individuals are depicted wearing shoes that have an open area over the foot and are closed by buttons at the ankle. King Josiah, on a window at Canterbury Cathedral dated to *c.*1200, is shown wearing such shoes (Zarnecki *et al.* 1984, 60, No. 93), as is the figure of Aminadab on the west window of the same cathedral, dated *c.*1180–1205 (*ibid.*, 144–5, No. 94a). A low-cut shoe from London, with an opening over the instep as on a modern bar shoe, can be seen in Fig. 10 (p. 12), but this was probably fastened with a drawstring. Buttoned – that is, toggle-fastened – shoes do occur within the present collection but not until the late 13th century, and then without open areas over the foot. Whereas manuscripts show mainly buttoned shoes, low boots, and slip-on shoes, the excavated shoes are predominantly drawstring, a type which remains unidentified in manuscript illustrations. The low boots, however, which feature prominently in these illustrations, form approximately one third of each of the early excavated groups (see above, Tables 1 & 2). The collection contains only one decorated 13th-century shoe (Fig. 115a and pp. 79–80) – which may be an example of what was being worn at this time by the wealthier sectors of society – but funerary monuments, such as the tomb of Henry III (Fig. 153), indicate how elaborate such footwear could be.

Before 1300, to judge by illustrative evidence, boots seem to have been the most common form of footwear, and this impression is reinforced by the 13th-century material in the collection, amongst which boots and ankle-shoes predominate. After *c.*1300 boots in particular are shown exceptionally, and are mostly worn by mounted travellers and huntsmen. These boots were usually shaped to the leg, and fastened by lacing or buckles in the small of the leg. On looser boots, the fullness below the knee was caught back from the front to the outside of the knee and hooked or buckled down in a broad fold. The Merchant in *The Canterbury Tales* is described as having *His botes clasped faire and fetisly* ('elegantly') (ed. Skeat 1912, 273). More commonly, people are shown with low boots (Fig. 154) and buttoned shoes, although the shoes illustrated as buttoned are frequently open over the foot, which those in the present collection are not (see above, pp. 21–2).

By the 14th century, shoes shown in manuscripts seem to be simple in cut but richer in material and ornament than was seen previously. They may be embroidered or decorated in openwork with reticulated, diapered or floral designs, and it is probably no coincidence that most of the

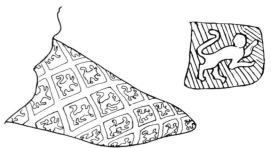

153 Detail of the shoes of Henry III, from his tomb in Westminster Abbey. The decoration, which consists of lions framed by lozenges, was probably embroidered.

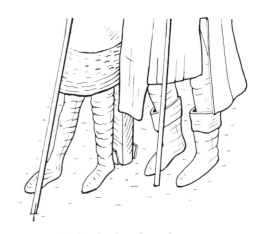

154 Detail showing low, loose boots.

155 Detail of the shoes of Edward III, from his tomb in Westminster Abbey. The decoration consists of embroidered leaves divided into panels by a central stylised cross.

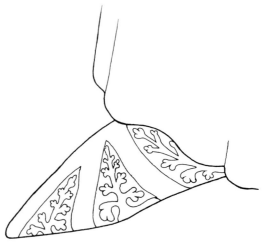

decorated shoes in the collection, except those with embroidered vamp stripes, are dated to late in this century (see above, pp. 80–7). The effigy of Edward III in Westminster Abbey wears shoes that are decorated – probably in imitation of embroidery – with panels of leaves separated by the arms of a stylized cross (Fig. 155). At the lower end of the social scale, Chaucer describes the parish-clerk Absolon in The Miller's Tale as having *Powles window* (viz. a window in St. Paul's Cathedral) *corven on his shoos* (ed. Skeat 1912, 3318). Indeed, drawings by Smirke of a wall painting once in St Stephen's Chapel at Westminster show one figure wearing shoes decorated with just such an architectural design – one reminiscent of the rose window of a Gothic cathedral (see Fig. 118; *cf.* Fig. 116c in the present collection and Baart *et al.* 1977, 75, No. 2). It is not clear, however, whether the artist has intended to show embroidery or, as on the other shoes in the same scene, openwork decoration.

156 Weeper from the tomb of John of Eltham (d.1337) in Westminster Abbey. The figure is probably wearing footed hose.

Hose fitted with soles seem to have been worn from the middle of the 12th century, if not earlier. Fig. 156, taken from the south side of the monument to John of Eltham, second son of Edward II (d. 1337), shows one of the weepers with what seem to be footed hose, shaped to the foot with only a slight point to the toe. Manuscripts show the majority of wearers of short tunics in long footed hose of stout woollen material or leather – King John had a pair of cow hide (Cunnington & Cunnington 1973, 31) – not joined at the top but held up by strings attached to the belt. The soles often had thin inner soles of leather or felted wool (Herald 1981, 212). Sometimes shoes were worn over the hose; sometimes short hose or buskins. One writer believes that the late 14th-century fashion for parti-coloured hose, coupled with the extreme toe lengths and the popularity of pattens, meant that shoes were seldom worn during the second half of the century (Yarwood 1979, 76). It is difficult to comment on this subject, since Yarwood's information comes from illustrative sources which mostly depict the fashionable upper and upper middle classes. The sources of the waterfront dumping in the City of London are most likely to be middle or lower class households, and probably for this reason tend to be at variance with the conventional, pictorial evidence. The late 14th-century deposits at 'Baynards Castle' produced the largest assemblage of shoes excavated in the City (possibly partly because of the excellent preservation on the site). And the 'Baynards Castle' and Billingsgate groups from this period yielded both shoes with extreme points and modestly-pointed shoes shaped to the foot (see above, pp. 29–31 and Table 8).

The adoption of sumptuous clothes and ostentatiously fashionable shoes served to reflect the growing prosperity of the middle classes. It is interesting to note that France, which shared England's prosperity during this period, also adopted 'poulaines', whilst in Amsterdam, which did not start to flourish commercially until the late 15th century, few 'poulaines' have so far been found on archaeological sites until that date (Jan Baart, pers. comm.). Excavated Swedish shoes, although displaying some similarity in fastening types to the London material, feature only modest toe shapes. Indeed, if they are dated correctly and are not residual, some of the 14th-century shoes from Lund seem still to have been fastened with the vertical and horizontal drawstrings long out-moded in England (Blomquist 1938, Figs. 28–47). The shoes from King's Lynn also present a differ-ent picture of 14th-century footwear. Here there were a few modestly-pointed shoes but no sur-viving 'poulaines' (Clarke & Carter 1977, Fig. 168, Nos. 63–4). Thornton reconstructed a shoe from Roushill, Shrewsbury that has parallels among the mid to late 14th-century two-piece shoes from London, but again it is neither a 'poulaine' nor even pointed (Thornton 1961, Fig. 53.1). 'Poulaines', some elaborately decorated, do survive from Coventry (Thomas 1980), but are datable only by style, not by context.

The chronicler who compiled the *Eulogium Historiarum*, probably at the very end of the 14th century, specifically attributed the first appear-ance of 'poulaines' – and of some other equally outrageous forms of dress – to the years 1361–2:

Eodem anno et in anno praecedenti tota communi-tas Anglicana versa. . . . Habent etiam sotulares rostratas in unius digiti longitudine quae 'Crakowes' vocantur; potius judicantur ungula daemonum quam ornamenta hominum. . . .

(v. 186; Haydon 1863, vol. iii, 230–1)

('In that year (viz. 1362) and the preceding year the whole of the English community was turned upside down. . . . They also have beaked shoes, one finger long, which are called "Crakowes"; they are judged to be the claws of devils rather than the trappings of men. . . .')

The exactitude with which this date is given imme-diately arouses suspicion, especially since in the same years England was shaken by a serious recurrence of the Black Death. Decadence and catastrophe may have been unconsciously linked in the chronicler's mind, just as in France in 1374 a new outbreak of plague brought on a resurgence of public hysteria fuelled by the feeling that demonic presences were poisoning society. Noth-ing pointed more surely to the Devil's handiwork than 'poulaines' which all had heard denounced so often by the clergy (Tuchman 1979, 260).

Stow, on the other hand, in his discussion of the Cordwainers' Hall in Bread Street ward, traces the introduction of 'poulaines' to 1382, stating that

Of these Cordwayners, I reade, that since the fift of Richard the 2. (when he tooke to wife Anne daughter of Veselaus King of Bohem) by her example the English people had vsed piked shooes, tied to their knees with silken laces, or chaynes of silver and gilt. . . .

(ed. Kingsford 1971, 351; repeated, *id.*, *A Summarie of the Chronicles of England* (1598), 149–50)

But since the latter part of this passage – regarding the tying of pikes to the knees with chains or laces – is almost certainly fictitious (see below), it may be that the first part should be regarded with equal suspicion. It is possible that Stow acquired the date from an authentic medieval source but more likely, perhaps, that it was an educated guess, made in the knowledge that the important cultural centre of Krakow – which gave its name to this particular type of shoe – lay less than a hundred miles from the border with Bohemia.

Whatever the precise date of the introduction of 'poulaines', archaeological and historical sources are consistent in demonstrating their popularity during the 1380s and, possibly, the 1370s. Their sheer impracticality and opulence was a natural target for anyone of sober tastes with an axe to grind – and in the years around the Peasants' Revolt there were many of these. William Lang-land, for instance, was never more than a poor chantry priest in the City of London. Here he must have seen many displays of conspicuous extrava-gance, not least among monks – even Franciscans by the 14th century – whose monasteries were supported by rich endowments. It is no surprise, therefore, that he should describe proud priests in the company of the Anti-Christ as wearing *pyked shoes* (*Piers Ploughman*, B.xx.218; ed. Skeat 1886, i.590); and, even if he did not write the passage himself, he would no doubt have agreed in condemning the Franciscans in the following terms:

*Fraunces bad his bretherne/barfot to wenden
Nou han they buclede schone/for blenyng of her heles
And hosen in harde weder/y-hamled by the ancle.*

(Anon., *Pierce Ploughman Crede*, 298–300; quoted in Fairholt 1885, i.135)

'Poulaines' achieved such notoriety, and were the butt of so much ridicule, that it is often difficult to distinguish fact from fiction. For example, the persistence of the idea that some were so long that they had to be tied to the knee (or waist) with chains seems to depend on just two scraps of secondary evidence: an 18th-century description (cited in Strutt 1842, ii.236 note 3) – apparently never substantiated since – of a painting of James I of Scotland, and statements by two late 16th/early 17th-century antiquarians, Stow (see above) and Camden (1614, 232–3). Stow gives no source but Camden specifically attributes his statement about 'poulaines' chained to the knee to the *Eulogium Historiarum*, even though when compared with the original text (reproduced above) his 'translation' of the same passage can be seen to be no more than a paraphrase with interpolations. It may be that his copy of the *Eulogium* had been annotated by later commentators – possibly in the medieval period – but until their authority can be confirmed it seems best to disregard these claims and to draw conclusions about the potential length of 'poulaines' from the shoes themselves. None of the shoes in the present collection extend more than 3–4 inches (75–100 mm) beyond the big toe (see above, Table 8), but even this would apparently have been prohibited by later sumptuary laws. Amongst the 14th-century shoes, pointed toes are common, if not universal, but the same cannot be said for the longer versions of this style.

'Poulaines' had passed out of fashion by 1400, if not earlier, and a more rounded toe style then

seems to have become popular. By the middle of the 15th century, however, they again returned to favour, and this time reached such extremes that sumptuary legislation was passed to prohibit their excesses. The intention was presumably to frustrate the flashy ambitions of the *nouveaux riches* and to conciliate the aristocracy, at a time when the king, Edward IV, most needed their support. First, when in 1463 it was enacted that *no Knight under the State of a Lord, Esquire, Gentleman, nor other Person shall use nor wear . . . any Shoes or Boots having pikes passing the Length of Two Inches. . . . (3 Edw iv c.5)*, the use of 'poulaines' was restricted to people of the highest rank; and then, in 1465, even this liberty was withdrawn, so that all cordwainers and cobblers within the City of London or its surroundings were forbidden to make shoes of any kind with pikes more than two inches long *(4 Edw iv c.7)*.

As for the other features of late medieval shoes, late 14th-century brasses of affluent members of the rising middle class show citizens mainly wearing shoes cut high at the back of the ankle with strapped – either strap and buckle or latchet – fastenings (Figs. 157–8). This impression seems

158 Detail from the brass of Robert Attelathe (d. 1376) in St. Margaret's Church, King's Lynn. His shoes are fastened with a strap and circular buckle. Note the long curving toes.

157 Detail from the brass of Robert Braunche in St. Margaret's Church, King's Lynn. The shoes have 'poulaines' and may be of the side-latchet type.

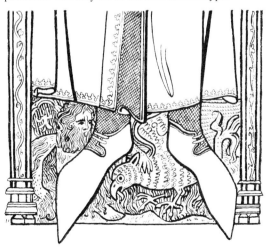

to be confirmed by the material from the late 14th-century dumps at 'Baynards Castle' in particular (see above, Table 6 and pp. 28–9), but it contrasts with sites on the Continent, notably Lübeck, where the dominant shoe types were low front-laced shoes with two pairs of holes, and front-laced ankle-shoes with five pairs of holes (Groenman-van Waateringe pers. comm.). Amsterdam also contrasts with London in the absence of low-cut strapped shoes, but the range of front-laced shoes is similar (*cf.* Figs. 56–7 with Groenman-van Waateringe & Velt 1975, 103, Abb. 5.4–5). The front and side-laced shoes in the London collection – except where there is continuous lacing – have paired holes which could be closed by latchets, (*cf.* Fig. 55); there are few examples with uneven numbers of lace-holes (*cf.* Fig. 58 with *ibid.*, Abb. 5.3). Fig. 27, dated to the early 13th century, closely resembles a 14th-century Dutch shoe (*ibid.*, Abb. 5.2): both are of one-piece 'wrap-around' construction, with triangular inserts, and have continuous side-lacing.

By the early 15th century, however, it is low side-laced ankle-boots that dominate both the archaeological assemblages and the brasses. An outstanding example of 15th-century footwear occurs on the brass of Nicholas Canteys (d. 1431) in Margate. Canteys wears low ankle-boots with a topband, embroidered decoration and continuous lacing up the side through seven pairs of lace-holes (Fig. 159). Except for the decoration, the style is very similar to the shoes from Trig Lane illustrated in Figs. 69–70, the dominant type in groups from this date. The brass of Thomas Bokenham (d. 1460), in St. Stephen's Church, Norwich, also depicts shoes reminiscent of those from Trig Lane, namely boots fastened at the ankle with what seems to be a pair of small buckles (Fig. 160; *cf.* Fig. 66). The general styling is similar, although the shoes on the brass, post-dating the excavated examples by some 20 years, are more pointed and reflect the return to fashion of the 'poulaine' in the mid 15th century.

Kelly and Schwabe (1972, 32) suggest that it was at this time that boot vamps started to be cut separately from the boot leg, and indeed in the present collection, the boots remain predominantly of one-piece, or 'wrap-around', construction until the early/mid 15th-century groups from Trig Lane. There are certainly numbers of low boots, and even boots reaching half-way between

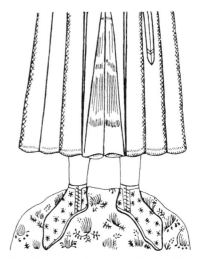

159 Detail from the brass of Nicholas Canteys (d. 1431) in St. John's Church, Margate, Kent. He wears embroidered ankle-shoes fastened by side-lacing. It seems that a single continuous lace was used.

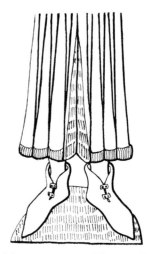

160 Detail from the brass of Thomas Bokenham (d. 1460) in St. Stephen's Church, Norwich.

the ankle and the knee, prior to the 15th century, but the total absence of identifiable fragments of higher boots is notable, even when the frequency of leather reuse is taken into account. Professor Groenman-van Waateringe has suggested (pers. comm.) that many of the vamps recovered in excavation may be from boots in which the vamp and the boot leg were separate pieces. However, the material from 'Baynards Castle', where there were large numbers of separate vamps and quarters, contradicts this theory, since on this site most of the shoes were virtually complete with little or no evidence of reuse. There remains the possibility that broad leather strips, which have been lost or reused, were sometimes added to heighten ankle-shoes that otherwise appear to be complete (*cf.* Fig. 23 and discussion, p. 50), but, this aside, the absence of full boots remains largely unexplained.

Pattens – wooden or leather overshoes fastened to the foot with leather cross-straps – came fully into fashion in the late 14th century and became virtually a staple element in 15th-century England (see above, pp. 91–101), just as on the Continent. Fifteenth-century illustrations, such as that reproduced here (Fig. 161), or the famous painting by van Eyck celebrating the Arnolfini marriage (now in the National Gallery, London), often show pattens raised from the ground on 'wedges' (*cf.* Fig. 127), a style absent from all the London groups of this period. The pattens in the van Eyck painting, dated 1434, already have long pikes, either because the Low Countries anticipated England in its readoption of this style in the 15th century or, perhaps, because in Europe there was no real break in the popularity of 'poulaines' from the end of the 14th century onwards. The latest pattens from the London excavations all have rounded toes, to match the contemporary shoes, but several in the established Museum of London collection may belong to the time of the pike's return to favour in England in the late 1450s or 1460s. One has an all-leather composite sole (Guildhall Museum 1903, Pl. lxxvi.7; cf. Figs. 139–40), but another has a hinged wooden sole which shows an improvement on the plain butted joint found at 'Baynards Castle' and Trig Lane (Fig. 133), in that one section of the sole is lapped over the other to make the joint more watertight (*ibid.*, Pl. lxxvi.5).

Status

The issue of status is an intriguing one, and could account in many instances for the seeming discrepancy between what is shown in contemporary illustrations and the pattern shown by material from archaeological sites. The waterfront dumps in the City of London, despite extensive study,

have revealed little about the sources of the rubbish deposited therein. Status is much easier to discuss if the shoes are associated with specific dwellings. Yet contemporary illustrations seem to use different types of footwear to denote differences both in status and role. Frequently on 11th/12th-century manuscripts, a king or central figure is shown wearing shoes decorated with vamp stripes, surrounded by figures wearing undecorated, undyed ankle-shoes. Yet the high proportion of shoes with such decoration in the present collection makes it unlikely that much significance should be attached to the presence of these shoes in the London groups. Manuscripts consistently show the central crowned figure wearing buttoned shoes whilst other figures wear simple slip-on shoes cut either at or just below the ankle. Given the 14th-century reaction to the presumptuous attire of the middle class, it is safe to assume that the possession of shoes like those in Fig. 48 was an indication of some status. With other shoes and shoe styles it is more difficult to tell. A pair of undecorated side-laced shoes excavated in the Løm stave church in Norway and dated to the late 12th or early 13th century have been identified by Schia (1977, 148) as the property of a member of the upper class because of their association with spun gold threads. The shoes are very similar to those shown in Figs. 27–28, which, simply on the basis of style and without other association, would not be considered objects of particular status.

161 Detail of pattens and 'poulaines'. 15th-century.

Invoices and inventories give some idea of what the wealthier members of society were wearing as well as what they were paying for their shoes. For example, we read:

> *To Robert le Fermor, bootmaker of Fletestreet, for six pair of boots with tassels of silk and drops of silver-gilt, price of each pair, five shillings, bought for the King's use. Westminster, 24th of May. 1 l 10 s.*

(Wardrobe accounts of the 14th year of Edward II (1320–1); *Archaeologia* xxvi (1836), 344–5)

The shoes of the common people do not seem to have been expensive items to make. Salzman listed the prices for piecework in Bristol in 1364 as threepence for making a pair of boots in their entirety: that is, a penny for cutting and twopence for sewing. Twopence was the payment for cutting one dozen shoes – a penny for all the uppers and a penny for the soles – with a further penny for lasting (Salzman 1923, 256). In the 13th and 14th centuries the average price of a pair of shoes, such as might be distributed charitably by the king to the poor, seems to have been about fivepence or sixpence (Mander 1931, 5–7) – roughly equivalent to a day's wages for a skilled labourer in the 14th century.

The Royal Wardrobe accounts contain a number of shoe-names, each presumably identifiable to contemporary readers as specific types, and these provide an idea of the variation that was possible. A requisition by Edward IV in 1480, for instance, includes the following items:

> *To Petir Herton cordewaner for a pair of shoon double soled of blac leder not lined price v d; . . . for a pair shoon of Spanish ledre single soled v d. each pair; for xj pair sloppes . . .* (of various types of leather) *. . . price of every payre xviij d . . . to Thomas Hatche for two pair of slippers price the pair vijd . . .* (to Peter Herton) *. . . for ij pair patyns of leder price the pair xijd. for a pair of Botews of tawney Spaynyssh leder price xvjd. for vij pair Botews of blac leder above the knee price of every pair iiij s . . .*

(ed. Nicholas 1830, 118–9)

Almost certainly some of these, such as the 'shoon', the 'botews' (but not the boots reaching above the knee) and the leather 'patyns', will have

been very similar to items in the present collection, but others – in particular, the 'slippers' and 'sloppes' – are not so readily identified. It is worth noting that by the end of the 15th century it was possible to specify 'double soles' – presumably 'turn-welt' or welted shoes – and that, as might be expected, the king would enjoy a much greater variety of leathers and finishes than is found in the normal archaeological assemblage.

Continental evidence similarly suggests that status is a factor which should be considered in the study of medieval footwear. Excavations in the towns of Dordrecht and s'Hertogenbosch in the Netherlands both yielded the same types of shoes, but in the former, more affluent town, the shoes were decorated and barely worn when discarded, while in the latter, less affluent town, they were plain and heavily worn (O. Goubitz pers. comm.). Goubitz interprets the contents of a cess pit in Deventer as representing the footwear of an entire household. Shoes were found in sizes probably representing the parents and children, along with other shoes in the same sizes with the quarters cut off so that they could be worn as mules: the shoes of the owners cut back and reused by the family retainers (O. Goubitz pers. comm.). Many of the shoes in the present collection are heavily worn and cut up for reuse, and a large proportion exhibit signs of repair, especially to the soles (see above, pp. 89–90 and Tables 15–16). The description given by the Cunningtons of peasants' shoes reinforced at the toe and heel with extra thicknesses of leather (Cunnington & Cunnington 1973, 111) accords well with shoes such as these, which have repair patches at toe and heel to cover holes in the original soles (Fig. 123).

Women's and children's shoes

It is rarely possible when examining shoes to differentiate between those worn by women and those worn by men except by size (see discussion, above, pp. 103–5). Women are generally shown in contemporary illustrations either with their gowns completely covering their feet or with merely the toes protruding. Even Chaucer is of little help. He describes the Wife of Bath in *The Canterbury Tales* thus:

> *Hir hosen weren of fyn scarlet reed.*
> *Ful streite y-teyd, and shoos ful moiste and newe*
> (ed. Skeat 1912, 456–7).

The Carpenter's Wife in The Miller's Tale wore shoes *laced on hir legges hye* (ed. Skeat 1912, 3267), possibly similar to those shown in Figs. 39–40.

It seems likely that in the 12th and 13th centuries women often wore boots – perhaps the high ankle-shoes found so frequently in archaeological deposits of this period. In 1200, King John ordered four pairs of boots for his wife, one of which was to be lined with grey fur (*quattuor par[ia] botar[um] ad feminas q[u]ar[um] unum par f[u]rret[u]r de gris; Liberate Rolls*, 2 John; ed. Hardy 1844, 9), and a French writer of similar date states that the nuns at Montmartre were allowed boots lined with fur as a concession to the cold (Strutt 1842, 49). Yarwood (1979, 82) has suggested that women wore the same fashions as men but did not affect the same extremes, and there are occasional confirmations that this was indeed so. The brass of Lady de la Pole (*c.*1380), for example, shows long 'poulaines' peeking from under her dress (Clayton 1968, Pl. 7), although the problems of walking in them must have multiplied when one had to manage a full-length skirt as well. The sculpture from the tomb of Blanche de la Tour (d. 1340), which shows only the lady's toes protruding from under her skirts (Fig. 162), is typical of many of the depictions of women during this period. In the absence of evidence from contemporary English sources, it becomes necessary to look at evidence

162 Detail from the tomb of Blanche de la Tour (d.1340) in Westminster Abbey, showing her shoes peeking from under her skirts.

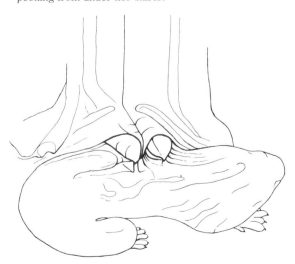

from the Continent, such as the illustration for February in *Les Très Riches Heures de Jean, Duc de Berry*. Here a shepherdess warming her feet against the winter's cold offers a rare display of ankles and feet, clad in modestly-shaped black (presumably undyed) ankle-shoes; her male and female companions wear buskins. An earlier 12th-century French feast scene, with male and female guests, depicts a tangle of feet under the table, all identical to each other (Cosman 1976, Fig. I.4).

Documentary sources confirm that young children wore shoes, though not perhaps that they wore them at so early an age as the archaeological finds imply (see above, pp. 104–5). The household accounts of Prince Henry, son of Edward I, list the shoes – including those worn at the King's coronation – that were purchased in 1273–4 for Henry himself, for his sister Eleanor, and for their cousin, John of Brittany (Johnstone 1922–3, 414–6). Henry was five or six at the time, and John was seven or eight. The shoes are merely described as *sotulares* (perhaps used here as a general term rather than specifically for below-the-ankle 'shoes'), and except for the information that some laces were purchased separately for Eleanor's shoes *(Item pro aguletis ad sotulares domine Alianore .j. d.)*, no details of styling are given.

Just over two centuries later, in 1478–9, Sir William Stonor was sent a bill by his shoemaker which specified, among other things,

> . . . *It. to my ladys chyldryn, xviij peyre, price of all the peyrys, iij.s.* . . . .

> (ed. Kingsford 1919, ii.74, No. 234)

The large number of shoes that were purchased on a single occasion for just four children – *my ladys chyldryn* were the three daughters and one son from Lady Elizabeth's first marriage – seems clear testimony both to the frailty of medieval footwear and to the rapidity with which children grow out of shoes. Archaeological excavations have yielded children's shoes in considerable numbers (see above, Table 19), though maybe not as many as might be anticipated. Even when no allowance is made for the distortion caused by a high rate of infant mortality, there are many possible practical considerations: that very young children went about barefoot, especially in the summer; that children wore footed hose or shoes and boots of undressed leather which would rarely survive on archaeological sites (Jan Baart, pers. comm.); that children's shoes were passed from the elder children to the younger; or simply that the children of the urban poor were less frequently provided with shoes than their counterparts in the great households, where servants and retainers were regularly issued with shoes and clothing. In London, as in Amsterdam, no children's boots were recovered, no decorated shoes and hardly any pattens. However, Cunnington and Buck (1965, 28) believe that children did wear pattens, and the single child's patten in the present collection (see above, p. 105 and Table 20) seems to support this theory, at least in part.

Manuscript illustrations and brasses offer comparatively little insight on this subject. Manuscripts overflow with barefooted Christ-childs which are not necessarily representative of the population as a whole, but one of the most lifelike manuscript images of a young boy – in the mid 14th-century Luttrell Psalter (Fig. 163) – clearly shows a front-laced shoe identical to those from 'Baynards Castle' (Figs. 53–4). It seems likely that there was a policy of dressing the child as a miniature version of his or her parent, and that this did indeed extend as far as the feet. However, the absence of shoes in the smaller sizes with extremely long toes (Table 8) and the absence of illustrations of children wearing 'poulaines' seems to indicate that children were exempted from the more extreme idiosyncracies of adult shoe fashion until the age of ten to twelve (de Neergaard 1985). Presumably, when Monstrelet wrote in 1467 of boys wearing 'poulaines' *on ell in length* (Fairholt 1885, i.181), he was referring to older children or adolescents rather than to infants.

Conclusion

Most of the conclusions about medieval shoe fashions reached over the past hundred years have been based on evidence from manuscripts and sculpture of the relevant period. Thus an opportunity to compare this work with surviving datable archaeological finds must not be overlooked. The evidence of the shoes in the present collection suggests that many of the conclusions about medieval shoes should be modified, or simply abandoned. The most obvious example of this is the occurrence of 'poulaines', not as the

standard footwear of the late 14th century but as exceptional. Indeed, drawstring shoes, which do not feature in manuscripts and are therefore largely overlooked by costume historians, occur extensively in London, as elsewhere in the country and on the Continent, and seem to constitute the main style of footwear for over a century. Perhaps Londoners were more susceptible than others to change in shoe fashion, since the drawstring seems to have been abandoned here some years before it was deemed unfashionable elsewhere. The alternative to this suggestion is that the close dating sequences of the London waterfronts make it possible to date these changes more closely than elsewhere, and thus that any discrepancies in dating are purely illusory. The range of high boots shown in manuscripts is totally absent from the London material, and this must reflect upon the frequency with which they were worn, and upon those who wore them. The range of decoration represented in the collection is more limited than evidence from manuscripts seems to suggest should be the case, and this again brings back the issue of the status of the wearers and the depositors of the waste along the Thames riverfront. The excavation of more specific sites – cess pits associated with dwellings, monastic sites and so on – might help to answer some of the remaining questions about the footwear of medieval Londoners.

163 Detail from the Luttrell Psalter (mid 14th-century) showing a young boy stealing apples. A pair of front-laced shoes has been discarded at the bottom of the tree. (See also half-title page)

Glossary

(see also, Thornton 1983)

Ankle-shoe	Item of footwear which extends to just above the ankle.
Boot	Item of footwear which extends considerably above the ankle.
Buskin	Low stocking of linen or silk. The term is sometimes used also for a type of high boot.
Clump sole	*see* REPAIR SOLE
Continuous lacing	Lacing with a single long lace, as opposed to several latchets.
Cordwain	Term properly used for leather from Cordoba in southern Spain. Originally made from sheep- or goatskin, later from cattle hide.
Decoration	*engraved:* executed with a blunt-edged tool.
	incised: executed with a sharp-edged tool.
	scraped: a thin layer of the grain surface of the leather is scraped away over an area to create a contrasting surface effect.
Drawstring	Fastening achieved by passing a leather thong either through a number of short paired slits in the shoe upper (Fig. 24) or through a series of vertical thongs (Fig. 15).
Flesh side	Original inner face of the leather.
Forepart	Front section of shoe or sole.
Grain side	Outer surface of the leather, originally bearing the wool, fur or hair.
Heel-stiffener	Piece of leather, usually triangular in form, stitched to the quarters on the inside for strengthening.
Insert	Piece of leather joined to the vamp or quarters to make up missing height or width (Fig. 164).
Instep	Upper surface of the foot between the rear of the toes and the ankle joint.

164 The main parts of a shoe.

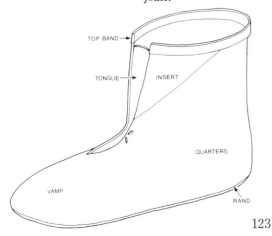

123

Lace	Long narrow strip, normally of leather, threaded through pairs of holes on opposite sides of an opening and pulled tight for fastening.
Lace-hole reinforcement	Strip of leather stitched onto the flesh side of the upper to strengthen the lace-holes (*cf.* Figs. 100, 108).
Lasting	Operation in which the upper is shaped around the last, a wooden block roughly matching the shape of the foot.
Lasting-margin	The part of the upper which is pulled onto the 'underside' of the last during lasting, and is later used to join the upper to the sole. The seam usually includes a rand, though not invariably before the 13th century. (*cf.* Figs. 72–4).
Latchet	In the present volume the term is used to denote a triangular split thong which is threaded through a pair of holes for fastening.
Patten	Used here as a general term for an item of open footwear made either as a platform of wood or as a stack of leather soles, and held on the foot by straps. Normally worn as an overshoe, but sometimes in the 15th century as a form of open sandal.
'Poulaine'	Also called 'Crakow', from a supposedly Polish origin, or 'pike'. Extremely narrow pointed toe, stuffed with moss or hair to hold the desired shape. Fashionable in the late 14th century, and in the middle of the 15th.
Quarters	The sides and heel of a shoe upper, which join the vamp on either side of the foot. In the strictest sense, quarters are seamed at the back of the heel, but in the medieval period most were made as a continuous section (Fig. 164).
Rand	Narrow strip of leather, triangular in section, sewn between the upper and the sole to make the lasting-margin more watertight.
Reinforcement cord	Cord secured by binding-stitch to vulnerable edges to provide added protection, for example on fastenings and along the vamp throat (Fig. 81).
Seams	*Butt seam* Join made by butting together the edges of two sections of leather and closing them with an edge/flesh seam (Fig. 77). *Overlapped seam* Join made by overlapping the edges of two sections of leather and sewing them together with grain/flesh stitches (Fig. 78).
Shoe	Item of footwear which does not extend above the ankle.
Sole	Underpart of shoe, usually of thicker leather than the upper. Almost invariably made with the grain side downwards. *Inner sole* Found in turn-welt or welted constructions (q.v.). Usually made with the grain side upwards. *Repair sole* Irregularly-shaped piece of thick leather stitched by loose tunnel-stitching to the main sole (Fig. 123). Sometimes known as a 'clump sole', which is perhaps to be preferred, since in the 15th century such soles occasionally seem to have been an original part of the shoe not a repair.

Stitching Usually done with plied, waxed flax.

Back-stitching Stitching done with a single thread that is worked forwards two holes and back one, so that a continuous row of stitches is left on the top surface (Fig. 138).

Binding-stitching Angled stitching along the edge of a piece of leather. Used for patching (Fig. 75), for joining two pieces edge-to-edge (Fig. 80) or simply to reinforce the edge.

Edge/flesh stitching Stitching from the flesh side of the leather through the edge and back. Used for attaching the sole to the upper (Figs. 72–3), and in most butt seams (Fig. 77).

Grain/flesh stitching Stitching through the thickness of the leather from the grain to the flesh side.

Tunnel-stitching Stitching in which the thread enters one side of the leather (usually the flesh side), passes through its thickness and then emerges on the same side. Used for attaching clumps to soles (Fig. 123).

Tongue Insert used to cover an opening at the vamp throat (Fig. 164).

Topband Narrow strip of leather or other material stitched to the top edge of a shoe, ankle-shoe or boot. Sewn in place by binding-stitch, leaving a characteristic scalloped edge on the upper (Fig. 164).

Turn-shoe Shoe constructed inside out and then reversed – or 'turned' – so that the seams and much of the stitching are on the inside (Figs. 72–3).

Turn-welt Strip of leather, wider than a rand, with two parallel rows of grain/flesh stitches. Transitional method of construction between the turn-shoe and the welted shoe. The upper, inner sole and turn-welt are sewn as for a turn-shoe, but the turn-welt extends outside the lasting-margin for attachment to a second, outer sole (Fig. 74).

Upper Parts of a shoe covering the upper foot and consisting of vamp, quarters and, possibly, inserts. Usually of finer leather than the sole, and made with the grain side upwards. Joined to the sole at the lasting-margin.

Vamp The front section of the shoe upper (Fig. 164).

Vamp throat Central portion of the rear end of the vamp, resting on the instep.

Vamp wing Sides of the vamp extending backwards on either side of the throat to join the quarters.

Waist Narrowest central part of the sole.

Welt A strip of leather wider than a rand with two parallel rows of grain/flesh stitches. The welt is stitched into the lasting-margin between the upper and the inner sole, with one edge protruding between the two. This edge is then joined to the outer sole using a grain/flesh stitch. The main difference from the turn/welt method of construction (q.v.) is that the shoe does not require turning.

List of figures and concordance

Except for the fragments shown in Fig. 116, all the illustrated shoes are from recent excavations. At present they are stored and catalogued by site, so that three items of information are required to identify a given object: the *site code* (TL 74, BIG 82 etc.; see below, Appendix 1), the *archaeological context number* (in square brackets) and the *accession number* (in triangular brackets; a continuous sequence of numbers, unique within each site). The date appended to each entry is, in every case, the date at which the layer containing that object is thought to have been deposited (Appendix 1). Those items which were submitted for identification of the wood or leather are marked with an asterisk, together with a brief note of the result. Further information about the leather types may be found in the archive report (Edwards 1986), which is permanently stored in the Museum of London.

*67 Adult's boot. Sole: cattle. Upper: calf. Heel-stiffener: probably calf. TL 74 [275] ⟨3278⟩, Group G15, *c.*1440.

*68 Child's boot. Sole: cattle. Upper: calf. TL 74 [368] ⟨1494⟩, Group G15, *c.*1440.

*69 Adult's ankle-shoe. Sole: cattle. Upper: ?deer/sheep/goat. TL 74 [275] ⟨2005⟩ ⟨2010–11⟩, Group G15, *c.*1440.

*70 Adult's boot. Sole: cattle. Upper: calf. Lace-hole reinforcement: probably calf. TL 74 [275] ⟨3324⟩, Group G15, *c.*1440.

71 Shoemakers at work (from *Das Hausbuch der Mendelschen Zwölfbrüderstiftung zu Nürnberg*).

a: Cutting out. Merdein Swob, dated 1459. (Drawn from Treue *et al.* 1965, Taf. 122)

b: Use of the awl. Hermann Schuhster, 1425. (*ibid.,* Taf. 34)

c: Stitching. Niclas Altreuss (cobbler), 1425. (*ibid.,* Taf. 259)

d: Trimming. ? Schuhster, 1432. (*ibid.,* Taf. 260)

72 Turn-shoe construction without rand.

73 Turn-shoe construction with rand.

74 Turn-welt construction.

75 Binding-stitch.

76 'Poulaine' sole, showing stitching at the toe. BC 72 [55] ⟨1669⟩, dock infill, 1375–1400.

77 Edge/flesh butt seam.

78 Overlapped seam.

79 Bevelled seam.

80 Butt seam with binding-stitch.

81 Shallow binding-stitch, securing reinforcement cord.

*82 Cutting pattern, early/mid 12th-century ?ankle-shoe. See Fig. 4.

*83 Cutting pattern, early/mid 12th-century ankle-shoe. See Fig. 5.

*84 Cutting pattern, early/mid 12th-century ankle-shoe. See Fig. 6.

*85 Cutting pattern, early/mid 12th-century embroidered ankle-shoe. See Fig. 7.

*86 Cutting pattern, early 12th-century embroidered ankle-shoe. See Fig. 8.

*87 Cutting pattern, late 12th-century boot. See Fig. 13.

*88 Cutting pattern, early 13th-century ankle-shoe. See Fig. 21.

*89 Cutting pattern, early 13th-century ankle-shoe. See Fig. 28.

*90 Cutting pattern, early 13th-century ankle-shoe. See Fig. 27.

*91 Cutting pattern, mid 13th-century ankle-shoe. See Fig. 33.

*92 Cutting pattern, late 13th-century ankle-shoe. See Fig. 32.

*93 Cutting pattern, late 13th-century boot. See Fig. 34.

*94 Cutting pattern, mid 14th-century shoe. See Fig. 36.

*95 Cutting pattern, mid 14th-century shoe. See Fig. 37.

*96 Cutting pattern, mid 14th-century boot. See Fig. 38.

*97 Cutting pattern, mid 14th-century boot. See Fig. 39.

*98 Cutting pattern, mid 14th-century shoe. See Fig. 52.

*99 Cutting pattern, late 14th-century shoe. See Fig. 53.

*100 Cutting pattern, late 14th-century ankle-shoe. See Fig. 55.

101 Cutting pattern, late 14th-century ankle-shoe. BC 72 [150] ⟨3772⟩, dock infill, 1375–1400.

*102 Cutting pattern, late 14th-century shoe. See Fig. 43.

*103 Cutting pattern, late 14th-century shoe. See Fig. 46.

*104 Cutting pattern, late 14th-century shoe. See Fig. 49.

*105 Cutting pattern, early 15th-century ankle-shoe. See Fig. 63.

*106 Cutting pattern, early 15th-century ankle-shoe. See Fig. 66.

*107 Cutting pattern, early 15th-century boot. See Fig. 67.

*108 Cutting pattern, early 15th-century boot. See Fig. 70.

109 Method used to fix buckle to strap.

110 Buckles and strap-end:

a: lead/tin alloy with iron pin. TL 74 [275] ⟨2623⟩, Group G15, *c.*1440.

b: lead/tin alloy with iron pin. TL 74 [368] ⟨2608⟩, Group G15, *c.*1440.

c: tinned iron. SWA 81 [2102] ⟨800⟩, *c.*1400.

d: lead/tin alloy with iron pin. TL 74 [368] ⟨2056⟩, Group G15, *c.*1440.

e: lead/tin alloy with iron pin. TL 74 [275] ⟨2507⟩, Group G15, *c.*1440.

f: lead/tin alloy with iron pin. TL 74 [275] ⟨2013⟩, Group G15, *c.*1440.

g: lead/tin alloy with iron pin. TL 74 [368] ⟨3432⟩, Group G15, *c.*1440.

h: lead/tin alloy with iron pin. SWA 81 [2102] ⟨850⟩, *c.*1400.

i: copper alloy with iron pin. TL 74 [368] ⟨3424⟩, Group G15, *c.*1440.

j: tinned iron. TL 74 [368] ⟨3638⟩, Group G15, *c.*1440.

111 Upper with embroidered decoration. SWA 81 [3015] ⟨4369⟩, mid/late 12th century.

112 Embroidered vamp stripes:
*a–b: Probably calf. BIG 82 [7005] ⟨5836⟩, Period IV.5, late 11th/early 12th century.
*c: Calf. SWA 81 [2167] ⟨4710⟩, undated.
d: BIG 82 [7064] ⟨4829⟩, Period IV.5, late 11th/early 12th century.
e: BIG 82 [6747] ⟨5954⟩, Period VII.2, *c.*1150–60.
f: BIG 82 [7064] ⟨4830⟩, Period IV.5, late 11th/early 12th century.
g: SWA 81 [3015] ⟨4372⟩, mid/late 12th century.

113 Embroidery stitches used on shoes.

114 Embroidered vamp stripe, stitches still surviving. SH 74 [451] ⟨207⟩, Waterfront I, *c.*1140.

115 Openwork decoration:
*a: Early 13th-century shoe. See Fig. 25.
*b: Upper fragment. Leather unidentifiable. BWB 83 [161] ⟨53⟩, *c.*1360–1400.
*c: Quarters. Calf. BC 72 [79] ⟨2338⟩, dock infill, 1375–1400.

116 Openwork decoration:
*a: Vamp. Calf. Museum of London 85.289/13. Probably from Billingsgate, ?late 14th century.
*b: Vamp. Calf. Museum of London 85.289/12. Provenance as last.
*c: Vamp. Calf. TL 74 [275] ⟨1834⟩, Group G15, *c.*1440.

117 Openwork decoration:
*a: Vamp. Calf. BC 72 [83] ⟨2557⟩, dock infill, 1375–1400.
*b: Vamp. Sheep/goat. BC 72 [79] ⟨2583⟩, dock infill, 1375–1400.

118 Detail of lost painting from St. Stephen's Chapel, Westminster. (Drawn by R. Smirke; copyright, Society of Antiquaries of London)

119 Late 14th-century shoes with incised and scraped decoration:
*a: See Fig. 51.
*b: Calf. BC 72 [79] ⟨2581⟩, dock infill, 1375–1400.

*120 Late 14th-century shoe with incised and scraped decoration. See Fig. 50.

121 Scraped and/or engraved decoration:
a: Vamp. BC 72 [88] ⟨1989⟩, dock infill, 1375–1400.
b: Vamp. BC 72 [79] ⟨2494⟩, dock infill, 1375–1400.
*c: Quarters. Calf. BC 72 [79] ⟨2337⟩, dock infill, 1375–1400.
*d: Quarters. Calf. BC 72 [79] ⟨2582⟩, dock infill, 1375–1400.

*122 Late 14th-century shoe with moss *(thuidium tamarascinum)* stuffing. See Fig. 49.

123 Method used to attach repair piece (clump) to sole.

124 Kurtz Franck, pattenmaker, at work, 1489 (from *Das Hausbuch der Mendelschen Zwölfbrüder-stiftung zu Nürnberg;* drawn from Treue *et al.* 1965, Taf. 164).

125 Wooden pattens, 13th/14th century. See Figs. 126 & 127.

*126 Patten. ?*Alnus* sp. SH 74 [467] ⟨362⟩, Waterfront III, *c.*1210.

127 Patten. BWB 83 [142] ⟨35⟩, 1360–1400.

*128 Patten. *Salicaceae.* BWB 83 [150] ⟨46⟩, 1360–1400.

129 Patten. BC 72 [88] ⟨3065⟩, dock infill, 1375–1400.

130 Patten. BC 72 [80] ⟨2061⟩, dock infill, 1375–1400.

131 Patten. BWB 83 [110] ⟨58⟩, 1360–1400.

*132 Late 14th/early 15th-century pattens. See Figs. 133, 136 & 139.

*133 Patten. Two parts, apparently conjoining, but identified as *alnus* sp. (⟨1607⟩) and ?*salicaceae* (⟨2684⟩). BC 72 [55] ⟨1607⟩ & ⟨2684⟩, dock infill, 1375–1400.

*134 Patten. *Alnus* sp. BC 72 [55] ⟨2520⟩, dock infill, 1375–1400.

The excavations

The footwear described in this volume came from ten separate excavations conducted during a period of just over ten years. A brief description of each of them is relevant not only as general background but as a specific guide to interpretation. The nature and scope of each site – whether a small 'watching brief' or a major area excavation – and inevitable differences in the condition of the leather and in the recovery methods have subtly biased the collection as a whole, giving rise to many small anomalies. It is immediately obvious, for example, that there are relatively few early 14th-century shoes, at least in comparison with the total from the second half of the century. This is not because there are fewer early 14th-century

sites – indeed, there are more – but because on one of them (Custom House) the areas opened were very small, on another (Trig Lane) the organic deposits of this date were very poorly preserved, and on yet another (Dowgate) only a limited 'watching brief', rather than a formal excavation, was possible.

Information about the size of each group, its condition and the method of conservation is provided in Table 21. The groups themselves have been variously dated by dendrochronology, associated datable objects (coins, pottery, pilgrim souvenirs) and, occasionally, historical or documentary references. The main arguments are summarised below, but for full details the reader is

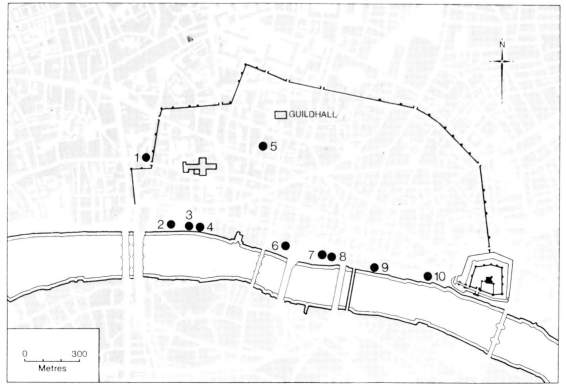

165   Plan of the City of London, showing sites excavated.

Table 21. Summary of the main groups of footwear from excavations in the City of London.

Site	Site phase	Date (century)	Registered shoes	Wood pattens	Leather pattens	Condition	Conservation method
Seal House	Waterfront I	early 12th	8	1	—	good	freeze-drying/solvent-drying
Billingsgate	Period VII	mid 12th	13	—	—	average	freeze-drying
Seal House	Waterfront II	late 12th	10	—	—	average	freeze-drying/solvent-drying
Billingsgate	Period VIII	late 12th	28	—	—	poor	freeze-drying
Milk Street	Pit 81	late 12th	3	—	—	average	freeze-drying/solvent-drying
Seal House	Waterfront III	early 13th	21	1	—	good	freeze-drying/solvent-drying
Billingsgate	Periods IX–XI	early 13th	38	1	—	average	freeze-drying
Seal House	Waterfront IV	early/mid 13th	9	—	—	average	freeze-drying/solvent-drying
Swan Lane	—[1]	mid/late 13th	40	—	—	average	freeze-drying
Billingsgate	Period XII	mid/late 13th	16	—	—	poor	freeze-drying
Trig Lane	Groups 2/3	late 13th	17	—	3	poor	mainly solvent-drying
Ludgate	ditch infill	early 14th	26	—	—	poor	freeze-drying (LUD 82) solvent-drying (LH 74)
Custom House	Groups C1/C2	early/mid 14th	4	1	—	average	solvent-drying
'Baynards Castle'	dock construction	mid 14th	41	—	—	very good	solvent-drying
Trig Lane	Group 7	mid 14th	6	6	3	poor	mainly solvent-drying
Dowgate	—	mid 14th	9	—	—	average	unconserved/treated with castor oil
'Baynards Castle'	dock infill	late 14th	417	12	—	very good	solvent-drying
Trig Lane	Group 11	late 14th	70	4	3	poor	mainly solvent-drying
Billingsgate	—[1]	late 14th	—[2]	15	—	average	freeze-drying
Swan Lane	—[1]	early 15th	16	—	1	average	freeze-drying
'Baynards Castle'	tower construction	early/mid 15th	6	1	4	average	freeze-drying
Swan Lane	—[1]	early/mid 15th	109	2	25	average	freeze-drying
Trig Lane	Group 15	early/mid 15th	359	13	143[3]	average	mainly solvent-drying

Notes:

(1) site phasing in progress;

(2) excluded from this volume;

(3) includes 128 unconserved 'bulk' fragments which were not individually recorded during the excavation and probably represent no more than 20 complete pattens.

referred to Vince (1985). Further information about the sites themselves is available in the *DUA Archive Catalogue* (Museum of London, 1986) or in the separate publications as listed. The site code, appended in parentheses after the full name of each site, is used in the *List of Figures and Concordance* (pp. 126–30).

1–6 Old Bailey/42–6 Ludgate Hill, EC4, 1982 (LH 74/LUD 82; Fig. 165.1)

Several sections were cut across the City ditch at Ludgate, showing it to have been recut several times in the late Saxon and medieval periods. The 26 registered shoes, together with a very large number of other finds, were all found in the latest of the ditches, which had apparently been levelled with rubbish in a single operation – certainly by 1340, when a row of houses was built on top, and possibly as early as *c*.1302–10, if a coin of this date was lost when freshly minted.

Baynards House, Queen Victoria Street, EC4, 1972 (BC 72; Fig. 165.2)

The excavation commonly known as 'Baynards Castle' covered an enormous area over 100 m wide to the south of Upper Thames Street (Webster & Cherry 1973, 162–3 & Fig. 60). This is considerably to the south of the original Baynards Castle, which was built by William I and apparently destroyed in the late 13th century. No trace of this or any other royal structure was found. The principal surviving remains were of 14th-century date: on the west, a series of timber and stone revetments and a stone-walled inlet or dock leading to a public watergate and, on the east, the walls of an adjoining private property. This property, which was examined further in 1981 (see below), was substantially rebuilt in the 15th century, and itself became known from that time onwards as 'Baynards Castle'.

The footwear described in this volume was all found in the vicinity of the 14th-century watergate inlet and may be divided into two groups.

(i) A small group of 41 registered shoes was found in dumps deposited at the time when the inlet itself was constructed. This is dated by pottery and jettons, probably to the second quarter of the 14th century.

(ii) A very large group (417 registered shoes and 12 pattens) was found among the enormous quantities of rubbish which were used to infill the dock in preparation for the southward extension of the watergate. Large groups of pottery, three coins, four jettons and several pilgrim souvenirs suggest that this was done in the last quarter of the 14th century. The preservation of leatherwork was better here than on any other site, mainly because of the depth of deposits in the dock and the presence of exceptionally large quantities of purely organic material. Different parts of the filling were examined in different ways, but in those areas which were most meticulously excavated – perhaps as much as half the total – it is likely that very nearly all the shoes originally present were recovered.

Baynards Castle/City of London Boys' School, Upper Thames Street, EC4, 1981 (BYD 81; Fig. 165.3)

Excavation exposed several successive timber and stone river walls, and part of the south-east corner tower of the 15th-century property known as 'Baynards Castle'. A very small group of 6 registered shoes and 5 pattens was found in layers deposited when the tower was constructed. Historical and documentary sources suggest that this was probably between 1428 and 1430.

2–3 Trig Lane, Upper Thames Street, EC4, 1974 (TL 74; Fig. 165.4)

The excavation extended over a very large area of *c*.450 sq m and revealed a complex sequence of revetments (G1–G15) ranging from the mid 13th to the mid 15th centuries; behind was a series of associated buildings (Milne & Milne 1982). Four major groups of footwear were found in the revetment dumps that were part of the four main stages of land reclamation.

(i) The earliest group, associated with the G2/G3 revetments, contains just 17 registered shoes. The reclamation dumps were excavated quite extensively, and large quantities of pottery were recovered, but it seems that either the dumps were composed of soil which contained few leather objects or that the conditions of preservation were so poor that few such objects have survived. The pottery, ampullae and a token suggest that the revetments were erected soon after *c*.1270.

(ii) The group associated with the second main revetment (G7) is similarly small and poorly preserved (6 registered shoes). In the absence of dendrochronological evidence and of intrinsically datable objects, a date of *c*.1340 has been proposed – mainly on the basis of the pottery and of estimates of the time taken for certain foreshore deposits to accumulate.

(iii) The third group appears to be slightly better preserved and consists of 70 registered shoes. The revetment with which it is associated (G11) has been dated by dendrochronology to *c*.1380, and this is supported by the evidence of jettons from the reclamation dumps behind.

(iv) The fourth group is by far the best preserved, and came from dumps behind the final – stone – revetment. These dumps covered virtually the whole area of the site and, since the volume excavated was probably at least twice that of any of the preceding dumps, a total of 359 registered shoes was recovered. The dumps themselves contained jettons and coins datable to *c*.1430–40, and the revetment rested on a timber with a dendrochronological date of *c*.1440.

1–6 Milk Street, EC2, 1976 (MLK 76; Fig. 165.5)
A series of Saxo-Norman buildings was uncovered, together with a large number of associated pits ranging in date from the 9th or 10th to the 12th or 13th centuries; above these was a sequence of later medieval stone buildings fronting Milk Street itself (Roskams & Schofield 1978). The only finds described in this volume are a group of three registered shoes from the latest of the pits (Pit 81). It is dated by pottery to the second half of the 12th century.

Public Cleansing Depot, Upper Thames Street, EC3 (Dowgate), 1959 (Fig. 165.6)
During observation on the east side of the Walbrook mouth, near the medieval Steelyard and public wharf of Dowgate, a clay river bank, probably of the late 11th or early 12th century, and one or more subsequent timber revetments were recorded. A small group of 9 registered shoes in dumps behind the latter was recovered in salvage conditions. Associated pottery suggests a date in the middle of the 14th century (*c*.1340–60).

Swan Lane/Upper Thames Street, EC3, 1981 (SWA 81; Fig. 165.7)
A small controlled excavation exposed a late 10th- or 11th-century clay bank, 12th/13th-century reclamation dumps and a series of hearths associated with the cloth-working industry. This

was followed by a watching-brief covering some 4,000 sq m, during which further dumps and revetments extending up to the early 15th century were observed. The footwear was nearly all salvaged during the watching-brief, in difficult conditions and may be divided into four groups.

(i) The earliest consists of just five registered shoes that were recovered from a series of deposits scattered across the site and associated with several different revetments. They are dated broadly to the second half of the 12th century by pottery and coins, although the same deposits also contain a large number of residual finds. For this reason, and because they have no cohesion as a group, the shoes have not been included in the general description of the collection (pp. 9–43); though the two with embroidered vamp stripes are considered in the detailed analysis of this type (pp. 75–9).

(ii) The second group (40 registered shoes) came from a series of large reclamation dumps which extended across the full width of the site, though the revetments associated with them were not fully recorded. The shoes were salvaged from a small area and presumably represent only a tiny proportion of the vast assemblages once present. This is unfortunate, because in terms of style the surviving group is one of the most homogeneous ever to have been found in London and it would be useful to know if this homogeneity originally ran through the group as a whole. A *terminus ante quem* of 1279 is suggested by the presence of 38 coins of Henry III and the absence of any attributable to Edward I's recoinage of 1279 itself. One of the coins can be dated to 1258 or later, but a pilgrim badge from Toulouse (1264 or later) and several badges thought to commemorate the centenary of Thomas Becket's martyrdom (in 1170) bring the *terminus post quem* forward, probably to 1270. A time in the 1270s can thus be suggested with some confidence.

(iii) The third group is again very small (16 registered shoes) and came from reclamation dumps contemporary with a further revetment. A timber from the revetment itself has been dated by dendrochronology to 1394 or later, providing a rough *terminus post quem*, and evidence from the immediately subsequent deposits (see below) suggests that this must, in fact, be very close to the actual date of construction.

(iv) The final group is by far the largest (109 registered shoes), but preservation was only moderate and there are very few complete shoes. It came from the foreshore and deposits in front of the revetment described above, and a sequence of 13 coins, including one from the last year of Henry V's reign, gives a *terminus post quem* of 1422. A large pottery assemblage, similar to that from Trig Lane G15 (see above), confirms this general dating.

Seal House, 106–8 Upper Thames Street, EC4, 1974 (SH 74; Fig. 165.8)

A long narrow trench, never more than 3 m wide, revealed three successive 12th- and 13th-century timber revetments, and the dumps behind a fourth (Waterfronts I–IV). Behind these lay a series of associated buildings (Schofield 1975). Groups of footwear were recovered from each reclamation deposit but, owing to the limited scale of the excavation, were only very small.

(i) A date of *c*.1140 is proposed for the earliest group (8 registered shoes), because dendrochronology has shown that timbers from the associated revetment were felled between the years 1133 and 1149. The deposit was apparently contaminated with a small amount of intrusive 13th-century pottery, but none of the shoes seem to be of so late a date.

(ii) The second group consists of 10 registered shoes, all in very bad condition. A date of *c*.1170 is likely for their deposition, since dendrochronology has given a range of 1163–92 for timbers from the revetment.

(iii) The third group is one of the most important from the whole London waterfront, because although quite small (21 registered shoes) it contains a high proportion of well-preserved complete shoes, including several types not found on other sites. Dendrochronology suggests a date of *c*.1210: a timber from the revetment gives a *terminus post quem* of 1193, and timbers from a drain cut through the bank some time after its construction give an estimated *terminus ante quem* of 1220.

(iv) The latest group (9 registered shoes) came from deposits for which pottery provides the only dating evidence; *c*.1250 seems most likely.

Billingsgate Lorry Park, Lower Thames Street, EC4, 1982 (BIG 82 (excavation); BWB 83 (watching-brief); Fig. 165.9)

Excavation covering 550 sq m showed that the area was first developed in the 10th or 11th centuries with the building of a stave-fronted clay bank which also revetted a small inlet. The bank was refurbished several times. Thereafter land was steadily reclaimed with timber revetments throughout the 12th and 13th centuries, but the rate of progress sometimes varied in accordance with the division between St Botolph's Wharf on the west and a row of private tenements on the east (Periods VII–XII). Behind the riverfront lay an undercroft and the church of St Botolph and, across a lane to the east, a series of commercial buildings which extended into the post-medieval period.

During the excavation up to a quarter of the soil in the reclamation deposits was finely sieved in order to recover environmental remains and small finds; and since not a single shoe was found by this process it seems certain that very nearly all the shoes originally present on the site were actually recovered. It is unfortunate, therefore, that with a few exceptions – all from the 13th-century deposits – they were poorly preserved and seem already to have been fragmentary when they were discarded. For present purposes they have been divided roughly into four groups.

(i) The earliest (Period VII), just 13 registered shoes, probably dates to *c*.1150 or a little later. Dendrochronology has shown that three timbers from the associated revetment were felled between the years 1144 and 1183 and the large pottery assemblage may be dated broadly to the mid/late 12th century.

(ii) The second group (Period VIII) consists of as many as 28 registered shoes, but all are very fragmentary. A date of *c*.1185 is suggested by the finding of a coin of Henry II (1180–9) and by the date of the following revetment (q.v.).

(iii) The third group, broadly datable to the first half of the 13th century, contains a total of 38 registered shoes from a series of three deposits which either accumulated in front of a major timber revetment or were associated with its construction (Periods IX, X, XI). A date of *c*.1210 can be proposed for the building of the revetment itself and for the primary deposits (Periods IX, X); dendrochronology gives a range of 1189–1234 for one of the timbers, and this seems consistent with a coin which has been provisionally identified as an issue of John (1205–16). A coin of Henry III (1223–43), however, gives a slightly later date to the deposits of Period XI, probably in the second quarter of the 13th century.

(iv) The final group (16 registered shoes) probably dates to *c*.1250–60. Three long-cross pennies give a *terminus post quem* of 1247–50, and this is confirmed by a large group of pottery and four 'D1' tokens – a type of which there were 94 examples in the 1270–9 group at Swan Lane.

During subsequent work by building contractors, after the formal excavation had been completed and when only limited access was possible, several 14th-century revetments were observed and groups of finds which are apparently consistent chronologically were salvaged *in situ* or from dumps tipped on and off-site. Among these are a significant number of shoes and pattens, almost all of late 14th-century date. The pattens are described in this volume (pp. 93–100), but the registered shoes have been excluded since they were recovered when writing was already far advanced.

Custom House, Wool Quay, Lower Thames Street, EC3, 1973 (CUS 73; Fig. 165.10)

Excavation in fifteen small dispersed trenches exposed two successive 14th-century timber revetments and, behind them, the foundations of the late 14th-century Custom House (Tatton-Brown 1974; 1975). The shoes have been published previously (Jones 1975) and, together with most of the other finds, came from reclamation dumps associated with the revetments. Only one group is described in the present volume – 4 registered shoes which probably date to the second quarter of the 14th century. They appear to come from deposits (Groups C1/C2) which were contemporary with a revetment dated by dendrochronology to 1318 or later and which were associated with early 14th-century pottery.

Conservation

Katharine Starling

See also Ganiaris *et al.* 1982; Starling 1984.

The nature of excavated leather

Leather is composed mainly of the protein collagen arranged in fibrils which, in turn, make up the random, fibrous network that gives it its characteristic elastic qualities. Tanning (see above, p. 46) retards the decay of collagen by inhibiting attack from many micro- and macro-organisms which may use it as a food source, and at the same time, to some degree, prevents chemical decay. Leather also contains fats and oils from several sources. Some may be from the original skin, although most of these will have been removed during tanning; some may have been deliberately worked into the leather to increase flexibility; and others may have been accidentally absorbed during use – body fluids, for instance – or, more rarely, during burial. The leather may also have been dyed.

Leather is not impervious to decay however, and will not survive unless the layers in which it is deposited exclude micro-organisms and the soil is not too acid or alkaline. The objects described in this volume were nearly all found in waterlogged or thick wet clay deposits where little or no air was present. Some of the tannins and fats will have been washed out during burial, others may have seeped in. Salts and decay products from associated materials and from the surrounding soil may have stained the leather. Some decay may have occurred. The history of the leather before, as well as after, deposition is always a factor, as is the type of leather used.

Associated materials

Conservation is made more difficult by the presence of other materials. These include metals, from buckles, strap-ends or decorative studs, and organic remains from stitching, textiles or the moss used for stiffening toes. Many pattens are made partly from wood, and the surface of leather may be decorated with gilding or painting.

Condition

The condition of the leather on excavation varied enormously (see above, Table 21). Some pieces were remarkably good, flexible with little sign of degradation, whilst others were hard, brittle or delaminating badly. There were sometimes considerable concretions of soil and metal corrosion products, especially if there were iron fittings.

Before conservation

Leather can be stored before conservation either wet or frozen. Before 1982 the shoes were kept wet in a solution of a recommended fungicide, sodium orthophenyl phenate (SOPP), in tap water in a heat-sealed polythene bag with as little air as possible. From 1982 on they were usually frozen. They were still kept in a heat-sealed polythene bag, but with only a small amount of water and no fungicide. A domestic chest freezer was used. The latter method has advantages in that it does not include the use of fungicide, which may be hazardous to humans and also interfere with analyses of dyes, fats, etc., and that it takes up considerably less space. Freezing does not appear to harm either leather or most associated materials, but if wood is present the object is stored wet, as its fragile cell structure may be damaged. If wet storage is only for a short period it may not be necessary to use a fungicide.

Choosing a conservation treatment

Excavated leather cannot easily be stored, handled or studied while it is wet. It is also vulnerable to deterioration. If simply allowed to dry in air it shrinks, hardens, buckles and tends to look dark. This is because the strong surface tension of water pulls the fibres together as evaporation occurs. Treatment consists of drying it by methods which leave it flexible, strong and not uniformly dark. Care has to be taken not to remove evidence of dyes, paints and finishes. The following factors were considered when evaluating which techniques to use:

(1) *Strength and flexibility*

These are important not only because they make the leather feel and look pleasant, but also because they make study and handling much easier and less likely to cause damage.

(2) *Size*

Leather almost always shrinks during drying. This is not by a uniform amount but varies from piece to piece. No conservation treatment prevents all shrinkage but a well-chosen one can minimise it. It is impossible to know what size leather should be and whether the excavated size was as when buried or was either swollen or shrunken. Sizes were recorded when wet and the aim was to preserve these dimensions as closely as possible.

(3) *Stability*

Once dry, the objects could still deteriorate. Added materials (dressings, plasticisers, backing materials, adhesives, etc) were chosen that were not liable to attack and/or decay.

(4) *Appearance*

It is impossible to say what excavated leather 'ought' to look like. Different tanning methods, dyes and finishes give different effects of both colour and texture, and leather will darken during use. It is tempting to feel that treatments leaving it light in colour are 'better', perhaps because this is furthest removed from the dark, wet state, but that is subjective. Successful conservation should result in a wide range of colours, including black.

(5) *Preservation of evidence*

Successful treatments not only preserve or recover size, shape, colour and feel but also any other evidence which might be present, even if not apparent to the naked eye, such as tannins, dyes and original dressings. Analytical methods are becoming more sophisticated and even the most fragmentary and decayed piece can hold useful and recoverable information.

The methods chosen (Table 21)

If it is just allowed to air-dry the shrinkage of leather is, to some extent, irreversible, as touching fibres may bond together. Two different conservation methods were used to circumvent this problem:

(1) *Solvent drying* (Rector 1975)

This method was used up to 1982. The water in the leather was replaced by another liquid of low surface tension (acetone or alcohol) which was then allowed to evaporate. Although shoes treated thus were generally flexible with only moderate shrinkage, the method did have disadvantages. First, the solvents could extract some of the remaining tannins, fats and dyes. Secondly, it could only be carried out in a work-place with adequate fume extraction. It was also very time-consuming. The initial capital outlay was small but the cost of solvents was high. For these reasons, from 1980, freeze-drying was increasingly used.

(2) *Freeze-drying* (David 1981; Watson 1981)

This is a gentle process. It has been in use increasingly in many laboratories in the last 12 years. Its main advantage is that there is little risk that materials will be extracted. It also puts minimal strain on delicate objects. Trials showed that the average shrinkage of the leather was less than during solvent drying (Table 22). In this method the leather is frozen and placed in a vacuum. This causes the ice formed to sublime – that is, the water is removed without going through a liquid phase. The initial capital outlay for freeze-drying equipment is high but running costs are fairly low and it is far less time-consuming than the solvent method. Since 1983 the Museum of London has owned a freeze-drier and most items are now dried in this manner.

Leather treated by removal of water alone can still be rather stiff and 'thin' and there may still be some cross-linking of fibres. To make it more flexible, give it a 'fuller' feel and reduce cross-linking, a plasticiser or lubricant is added either before or after drying. This also reduces further shrinkage. Up to c.1980 a dressing was applied to all the leather after drying, consisting of lanolin and a water-repellent in either trichloroethane or white spirit (Rector 1975). This resulted in flexible leather which looked and felt 'good' but the process was discontinued – both because shrinkage was found to be less if the plasticiser was added before the water was removed and the leather was therefore never in a dry, unplasticised state, and because the materials used might confuse subsequent analyses. Since 1980 all leather has been soaked in an aqueous solution of glycerol and/or polyethylene glycol 400 as recommended by several laboratories (David 1981; Watson 1981) before either method of drying. These are less likely to interfere with analyses.

Neither drying method will harm most associated materials, with the exception of wood, which should not be solvent-dried. If it can be carried out without damage, objects may be dismantled and the different materials conserved separately.

Reconstruction

Although most objects could be studied adequately without being reconstructed, it was essential to assemble a few for the purposes of photography and public display. The methods used were those recommended by the York Archaeological Trust (Peacock 1983). Only inert materials were used. Cellulose nitrate (HMG) and polyacrylate (PLIANTEX) were used as adhesives. Dyed and waxed linen thread, dyed crepeline and brown felt were used for stitching, backing and gap-filling.

Table 22 Shrinkage of freeze-dried and acetone-dried leather (shoes and other objects) from London sites. Each bar represents the range of shrinkage in one batch of leather.

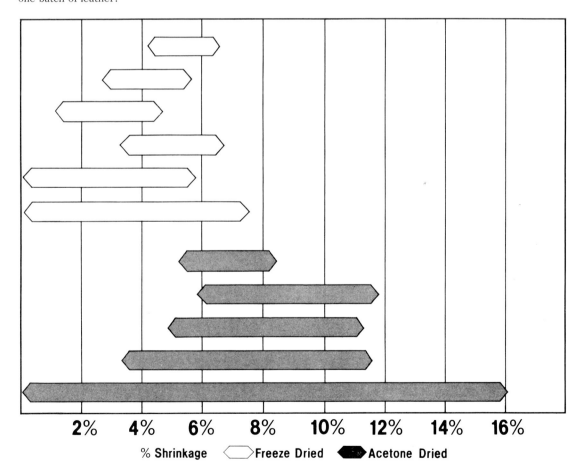

Bibliography

BAART, J, *et al.*, 1977 *Opgravingen in Amsterdam*

BAGLEY, J J, 1960 *Life in medieval England*

BLOMQUIST, R, 1938 Medeltida skor in Lund, *Kulturen*, 189–219

BRAUN, J, 1899 Der Paramentenschatz zu Castel S. Elia. Die Pontifikalsandalen und Mitren, *Zeitschrift für Christliche Kunst*, **10**, 291–302

BROBERG, B, & HASSELMO, M, 1981 *Keramik, Kammar och Skor från 7 medeltida städer*, Riksantikvarieämbetet och Statens Historiska Museer, rapport medeltidsstaden, **30**

CAMDEN, W, 1614 *Remaines concerning Britaine: but especially England, and the inhabitants thereof*, London

CHIBNALL, M (ed), 1969–80 Ordericus Vitalis, *The ecclesiastical history*, 6 vols

CHRISTIE, A B, 1938 *English medieval embroidery*, Oxford

CLARKE, H, & CARTER, A, 1977 *Excavations in King's Lynn 1963–70*, Soc Medieval Archaeol Monograph, **7**

CLARKS LTD, 1972 *Evidence from Clarks Ltd to the Munro Committee*, privately printed

CLAYTON, M, 1968 *Catalogue of rubbings of brasses and incised slabs*, Victoria and Albert Museum, London

COSMAN, M P, 1976 *Fabulous feasts*, London

COWGILL, J, DE NEERGAARD, M, & GRIFFITHS, N, 1987 *Medieval finds from excavations in London I: knives and scabbards*

CUNNINGTON, P, & BUCK, A, 1965 *Children's costume in England*

CUNNINGTON, C W, & CUNNINGTON, P, 1973 *Handbook of English medieval costume*, 2 edn

DAVID, A E, 1981 Freeze-drying leather with glycerol, *Museums Journ*, **81**, 103–4

FAIRHOLT, F W, 1885 *Costume in England: a history of dress to the end of the eighteenth century*, 3 edn, 2 vols

GANIARIS, H, KEENE, S, & STARLING, K, 1982 A comparison of some treatments for excavated leather, *The Conservator*, **6**, 16–23

GÓMEZ-MORENO, M, 1946 *El Panteon Real de las Huelgas de Burgos*, Madrid

GROENMAN-VAN WAATERINGE, W, 1974 Die Entwicklung der Schuhmode in 2500 Jahren, *Die Kunde* (n. F.), **25**, 111–20

———, 1975 Society . . . rests on leather, *Rotterdam Papers*, **2**, 23–34

GROENMAN-VAN WAATERINGE, W, & VELT, L M, 1975 Schuhmode in späten Mittelalter. Funde und Abbildungen, *Zeitschrift für Archäologie des Mittelalters*, **3**, 95–119

GUILDHALL MUSEUM, 1903 *Catalogue of the collection of London antiquities in the Guildhall Museum* (N.B. pagination differs in 2 edn, 1908)

HALD, M, 1972 *Primitive shoes*, Copenhagen

HARDY, T D (ed), 1844 *Rotuli de liberate ac de misis et praestitis regnante Johanne*, London

HARRIS, J, 1987 'Thieves, Harlots and Stinking Goats': fashionable dress and aesthetic attitudes in Romanesque art, *Costume*, **21**, 4–15

HAYDON, F S (ed), 1863 *Eulogium Historiarum*, 3 vols

HENDRIKS, A, 1964 Karolingisch schoeisel uit Middelburg, in J A Trimpe Burger, Een oudheidkundig onderzoek in de Abdij te Middelburg in 1961, *Berichten van de Rijksdienst voor het oudheidkundig bodemonderzoek*, **14**, 112–16

HERALD, J, 1981 *Renaissance dress in Italy 1400–1500*

JOHNSTONE, H, 1922–3 The wardrobe and household of Henry, son of Edward I, *Bull John Rylands Lib*, **7**, 384–420

JONES, J, 1975 Medieval leather, in Tatton-Brown 1975, 154–61

KELLY, F M, & SCHWABE, R, 1931 *A short history of costume and armour*, 2 vols

KINGSFORD, C L (ed), 1919 *The Stonor letters and papers 1290–1483*, London, 2 vols

———, 1971 John Stow, *A survey of London*

LATHAM, R, & MATTHEWS, W, 1970–83 *The diary of Samuel Pepys*, 11 vols

LONDON MUSEUM, 1935 *Costume*, London Museum catalogues, **5**, 2 edn

———, 1940 *Medieval catalogue*

MacGregor, A, 1982 *Anglo-Scandinavian finds from Lloyds Bank, Pavement, and other sites*, The Archaeology of York, **17**

Mander, C H W, 1931 *A descriptive and historical account of the Guild of Cordwainers of the City of London*

Mellor, J E, & Pearce, T, 1981 *The Austin Friars, Leicester*, CBA Res Rep, **35**

Milne, G, & Milne, C, 1982 *Medieval waterfront development at Trig Lane, London*, London Middlesex Archaeol Soc Special Paper, **5**

de Neergaard, M, 1985 Children's shoes in the thirteenth to sixteenth centuries, *Costume*, **19**, 14–21

Nicholas, N H (ed), 1830 *Privy Purse expenses of Elizabeth of York and wardrobe accounts of Edward the Fourth*, London

Peacock, E, 1983 The conservation and restoration of some Anglo-Scandinavian leather shoes, *The Conservator*, **7**, 18–23

Pritchard, F A, forthcoming Small finds, in A G Vince, *Aspects of Saxon and medieval London I: finds and environmental evidence*

Rector, W K, 1975 The treatment of waterlogged leather from Blackfriars, City of London, *Trans Museum Assist Group*, **12**, 33–37

Reed, R, 1972 *Ancient skins, parchments and leathers*

Rhodes, M, 1980 Leather footwear, in D M Jones, *Excavations at Billingsgate Buildings 'Triangle', Lower Thames Street, 1974*, London Middlesex Archaeol Soc Special Paper, **4**, 99–128

Richardson, K M, 1959 Excavations in Hungate, York, *Archaeol J*, **116**, 51–114

Roskams, S, & Schofield, J, 1978 Milk Street excavations: 2, *London Archaeol*, **3**, 227–34

Russell, J, 1939 English medieval leatherwork, *Archaeol J*, **96**, 132–41

Salaman, R A, 1986 *Dictionary of leather-working tools, c.1700–1950*

Salzman, L F, 1923 *English industries of the middle ages*

Schia, E, 1977 Skomaterialet fra 'Mindets tomt', in De archeologiske utgravninger i Gamlebyen, *Oslo* I, Universitetsforlaget, Oslo-Bergen-Tromsø, 121–201

Schmedding, B, 1978 *Mittelaltliche Textilien in Kurchen und Klostern der Schweiz*, Bern

Schofield, J, 1975 Seal House, *Current Archaeol*, **49**, 53–7

Skeat, W W (ed), 1886 William Langland, *The vision of William concerning Piers the Plowman*, Oxford, 2 vols

———, 1912 *The complete works of Geoffrey Chaucer*, London

Starling, K, 1984 *The freeze-drying of leather pre-treated with glycerol*, preprint 7th Triennial Meeting International Council of Museums Committee for Conservation, Copenhagen, **2**

Statutes of the Realm Record Commission, *The Statutes of the Realm*, 12 vols, 1810–1828

Strutt, J, 1842 *A complete view of the dress and habits of the people of England, from the establishment of the Saxons in Britain*, 2 edn (rev J R Planché), London

Stubbs, W (ed), 1889 William of Malmesbury, *de gestis regum Anglorum*, 2 vols

Swallow, A W, 1975 Interpretation of wear marks seen in footwear, *Trans Museum Assist Group*, **12**, 28–32

Swann, J, 1981 *Catalogue of shoe and other buckles in Northampton Museum*, Northampton

———, 1986 *Shoemaking*, Shire Publications

Tatton-Brown, T, 1974 Excavations at the Custom House site, City of London, 1973, *Trans London Middlesex Archaeol Soc*, **25**, 117–219

———, 1975 Excavations at the Custom House site, City of London, 1973: Part II, *Trans London Middlesex Archaeol Soc*, **26**, 103–70

Thomas, S, 1980 *Medieval footwear from Coventry*

———, 1983 Leather-working in the middle ages, in *Leather manufacture through the ages* (eds R Thompson & J A Beswick), Proc 27th E Midlands Industrial Archaeol Conference, 1–10

Thornton, J H, 1961 Report on shoe and other leather fragments, in P A Barker, Excavations on the town wall, Roushill, Shrewsbury, *Medieval Archaeol*, **5**, 205–6

———, 1983 *A glossary of shoe terms*, 3 edn

Treue, W, *et al.*, 1965 *Das Hausbuch der Mendelschen Zwölfbrüderstiftung zu Nürnberg*, 2 vols

Tristram, E W, 1944 *English medieval wall painting: the twelfth century*

Tuchman, B W, 1979 *A distant mirror*

Vigeon, E, 1977 Clogs or wooden soled shoes, *Costume*, **11**, 1–27

VINCE, A G, 1985   The Saxon and medieval pottery of London: a review, *Medieval Archaeol,* **29**, 25–93

WATSON, J, 1981   *Experimental assessment (1979) of freeze-drying techniques on waterlogged leather from seven London excavations – Part I,* Ancient Monuments Lab Rep, **3409**

WEBSTER, L E, & CHERRY, J, 1973   Medieval Britain in 1972, *Medieval Archaeol,* **17**, 138–88

YARWOOD, D, 1979   *English costume,* 5 edn, London

ZARNECKI, G, *et al.,* 1984   *English Romanesque art 1066–1200,* Arts Council of Great Britain

Summaries

Résumé

Lors des fouilles récentes entreprises par le Département d'Archéologie Urbaine du Musée de Londres, l'on a trouvé environ 1500 chaussures et socques datant de la période c.1100–1450. La plupart d'entre elles proviennent des remblais de la rive nord de la Tamise où elles ont été préservées anérobiquement, parce que saturées d'eau. L'étude dendrochronologique ainsi que les monnaies et la céramique ont permis de les dater assez exactement à un demi-siècle près.

Dans le premier chapître, *Chaussures des sites de Londres de 1100 à 1450*, on a voulu créer une typologie étendue à datation serrée, un moyen d'étude qui n'existait pas jusqu'à maintenant pour l'étude des chaussures de l'époque médiévale en Grande-Bretagne (voir aussi le tableau 1). Cette période a été divisée en sept sous-périodes, chacune durant cinquante ans environ, et les styles caractéristiques de chaque époque y sont décrits. Les meilleurs exemples de ces chaussures sont illustrés et sont représentatifs de chaque style, et le reste a été rassemblé sous forme de tableau.

Le deuxième chapître, *Fabrication et réparation de chaussures*, contient les analyses des fournitures utilisées dans la fabrication des chaussures: le cuir, le métal pour les boucles de chaussures et de lanières, et la mousse qui remplissait les bouts de chaussures. Les méthodes de fabrication et les types principaux de couture sont illustrés en détail; on y trouvera aussi un commentaire sur la décoration brodée, à jours ou gravée. Toutes ces indications prises ensemble montrent que, à Londres, vers le milieu du 14ème siècle, la fabrication des chaussures était une industrie de production de masse utilisant un nombre relativement restreint de motifs.

Dans le troisième chapître, intitulé *Socques*, l'on peut voir que les sur-chaussures en bois sont utilisées à partir du 12ème siècle sinon plus tôt, et que au début du 15ème siècle, un nouveau modèle avec une semelle en cuir est introduite. D'après le grand nombre de socques retrouvées, l'on peut dire que celles-ci étaient devenues très courantes et qu'on les portait simplement directement sur les bas comme des sandales ouvertes.

Dans le quatrième chapître, *Tailles et traces d'usures: indications sur la vie sociale*, on a voulu démontrer que bien qu'il n'est pas possible d'affirmer les tailles d'origine des chaussures de la collection, leur taille *relative* a été préservée. Ceci nous permet de distinguer, dans certains cas, les styles de chaussures d'hommes de ceux des femmes, et de voir que vers le milieu du 15ème siècle, il existait un type de chaussures spécialement conçu pour les jeunes enfants. Les déformités des pieds, comme par exemple les oignons ou les pieds rentrés en dedans, peuvent être également déduits à partir des traces d'usure que l'on voit sur les chaussures particulièrement bien préservées.

Une des plus importantes conclusions du dernier chapître, *Chaussures dans les arts et la littérature*, est que les bronzes de grande taille, les peintures et les illustrations de manuscrits, les sources habituelles pour l'étude des costumes médiévaux, ne sont pas toujours un guide sur lequel on peut compter en ce qui concerne les chaussures médiévales. Parfois, comme par exemple dans le cas de la mode des bouts pointus à la fin des 11ème et 14ème siècles, les sources archéologiques et historiques ou les illustrations concordent, mais le plus souvent il semble que les artistes se sont servis de conventions qui ne correspondent plus depuis longtemps avec la mode de l'époque. Cependant, lorsque l'on compare les chaussures provenant d'autres sites archéologiques sur le continent et en Grande-Bretagne, l'on peut voir que des modes de chaussures semblables s'étaient répandues dans l'Europe du nord-ouest. La collection londonienne avec ses dates proches les unes des autres et son excellente préservation, constitue une des plus importantes collections rassemblées jusqu'à présent.

Toutes les chaussures décrites dans ce volume sont au Musée de Londres, où elles peuvent être examinées sur demande écrite.

Zusammenfassung

In Ausgrabungen der Abteilung Urban Archaeology des Museums von London, wurden kürzlich beinahe 1500 Schuhe und Überschuhe aus der Zeit von ungefähr 1100–1450 gefunden. Die meisten lagen in Schichten, die zur Landgewinnung am Nordufer der Thames aufgeschüttet worden waren. Die luftdichte, wasserumschlossene Lagerung hat die Funde außerordentlich gut konserviert. Dendro- im Verbund mit Münz- und Töpferwaren-Chronologie machten es möglich, die Datierung auf 50 Jahre und kürzer zu begrenzen.

Das erste Kapitel, *Schuhe Londoner Ausgrabungen, von 1100–1450*, gibt erstmals eine eng datierte, breite Einführung in die verschiedenen Arten. Bisher war kein vergleichbares Material für das Studium mittelalterlicher Schuhe in Großbritannien vorhanden (Tafel 1). Der gesamte Zeitraum ist unterteilt in sieben Phasen von jeweils ungefähr 50 Jahren, für die die jeweiligen Modelle der Zeit beschrieben werden. Die am besten erhaltenen Beispiele sind stellvertretend für ihre Gruppe abgebildet, der Rest ist in Tabellen zusammengefaßt.

Das zweite Kapitel, *Schuhmachen und Schuhflicken*, setzt sich mit den Werkstoffen auseinander: dem Leder, dem Metal der Schnallen und Riehmenenden, dem Moos zum Ausstaffieren. Konstruktionsmethoden und die Hauptarten der Nähte sind mit detaillierten Abbildungen illustriert. Ebenso werden Stickereien, Lochornamente und Gravierungen gezeigt. Seit der Mitte des 14. Jahrhunderts wurden Schuhe in Massenproduktion unter Verwendung einer relativ kleinen Anzahl von Standardmustern hergestellt.

Im dritten Kapitel, *Überschuhe*, wird gezeigt, daß im 12. Jahrhundert, wenn nicht früher, hölzerne Überschuhe in Mode kamen. Im frühen 15. Jahrhundert wurde eine ganz neue Art Schuh mit einer zusammengesetzten Ledersohle eingeführt. Nach der hohen Anzahl der Funde zu urteilen, wurden lederne Überschuhe sehr populär, sie wurden über den Strümpfen als offene Sandalen getragen.

Das vierte Kapitel, *Größen und Tragespuren – soziale Rückschlüsse*, zeigt, obwohl es nicht länger möglich ist, die genauen originalen Schuhgrößen festzustellen, daß die *relativen* Größen noch vorhanden sind. Dadurch kann in einigen Fällen zwischen Männer- und Frauenstilen unterschieden werden. Außerdem erwies sich, daß um die Mitte des 15. Jahrhunderts eine besondere Art Schuh für Kleinkinder entwickelt wurde. Abnutzungsstellen an besonders gut erhaltenen Schuhen lassen auf Deformierungen von Füßen, sowie Entzündung der großen Zehe oder einwärts gerichtete Zehen schließen.

Eine der wichtigsten Schlußfolgerungen des letzten Kapitels, *Schuhe in Kunst und Literatur*, ist, daß figürliche Darstellungen auf monumentalen Messinggrabplatten, Gemälden und Manuskriptillustrationen, die traditionellerweise als Quellen mittelalterlicher Kostümstudien dienten, selten zuverlässig sind in Bezug auf Schuhzeug. Manchmal stimmen archäologische Beobachtungen und bildliche Darstellungen oder historische Quellen überein, wie zum Beispiel bei der Mode der langen Schuhspitzen des späten 11. bis späten 14. Jahrhunderts. Öfter hingegen scheint es daß die Künstler noch Moden darstellten, die im täglichen Leben lange überholt waren. Vergleiche der Funde mit anderen Ausgrabungen in Großbritannien und auf dem Kontinent zeigen, daß ähnliche Schuhmoden sich über ganz Nordwest-Europa ausdehnten, sodaß die Londoner Collection mit ihren genauen Daten und gutem Erhaltungszustand als eine der repräsentativsten und bedeutendsten Sammlungen erachtet werden kann.

Alle hier beschriebenen Schuhe werden im Museum von London aufbewahrt und können nach schriftlicher Anmeldung besichtigt werden.